smart enough to know that it was not about the knock down it was a about the get up. I don't care if you failed a 100 times as long as you get back up. Each time you get up it should make you stronger and stronger.

The stronger you get the better you will start to feel about yourself.

You will get to the point of no return, of no turning back. You will feel so great about yourself, you will realize that there is no stopping you now. I'm in control of my destiny I can choose the route I take from this point on.

People that feel good about there selves seem to live longer, there are stress free and know how to enjoy life. Why because they have something to live for. This can be you once you realize that your in control of your life. You know when people realize when they try to start there own business is not going to be easy. If you going into business for your self, you must all ready know this. If you don't you all ready starting off on your left foot. Pray that you can balance it out!

Unless you in inherited a business or have a lot of money, you are in for a up hill battle. Not saying you can't make it happen, that's not what I'm saying because I know you can. I just want to you know are you up for a battle, a battle you can and will win if you hang on.

I believe if we put God first in all we do we can make it. This a long should make you feel good about yourself, and you know that you are on your way.

Please don't give up or give in, you worked hard to get where you are dust far. If you hang on you have a better chance to get there. But if you quit you will spend the rest of your life wondering, what could have happen if I had a finish. Don't be this person.

CHAPTER II

HATERS

They are all around you in the home. In the church, friends ect. These are people that are afraid of there self. People that are scared to believe any thing they can't see. People that are with out faith. I hear people talk about going out on faith all of the time, but 98% of them are just talkers. There are as scared as a kid being left in the woods at night along.

Then there are some that have tried to get out of the every day worked force and it didn't work for them. So what they do every time you talk about doing something different they are the first to tell you it want happen, and what happen you believe the hype and give up. You can't and shouldn't let no one else failure become your future.

You should believe in you not in some one else that don't have faith in there self. You have your own life to live, take the challenge take the plung, go ahead you'll like it.

I mean just knowing that you step out side the box should make you feel good all by itself. Now that you are out run around and have some fun. Try and see what this world really have to offer you. Say to your self I'm free now. Don't hate me because I'm trying to live, but hate your self because you are not!

Some of the most miserable people in the world are haters, because they really don't know what to do with there life. In most cases they have all ready screwed up, there life and working on yours and whom every may work with them.

If they were smart enough to make a sound decision and stayed with it they would have been all right. But now we both know that sound anything is not what they do.

Sometimes when you think about making a career move it just best to keep it to your self, there fore there be no road blocks from the haters. It's time to set your self free, it's time to stop being a dream builder for some one else and start building your dreams. Some time you have to let go of your friends that stand in the way of process. May hurt may not who cares I don't, you may think, I'm hard but I'm just real. When you are tired as I am, of being broke, being with out, have to borrow for this and that. And when you get to the point your momma hate to see you coming it's time for a change. And getting rid of the hatter should be your first change. I tell people now to get out of my way. I'm going to the top with or with out you.

I'm coming threw, so move out of the way.

Haters beware! When people like that want to talk to you about your life. Have little to say about anything and soon they will leave. Some times it just best not to say anything.

Silent is like kryptonite to them they have to move on cause there is nothing for them to feed off of. Silence make them weak, they have nothing at all to fed off of. People like this need a light into your life. Don't light the candle, turn on the light switch, nor let up the shade. Keep these fools in the darkness, about your dreams and what you wanna do or doing and they will go away way. I PROMISE try it and see only a fool talks to them self. And if you really want get rid of them tell them Jesus said! Watch the demon run. lol

CHAPTER III

ONLY THE STRONG SURVIVE

Jan. 06, 2014

If you are weak you want make it, so there no need to fake it! And that what a lot of people do. This is why they never make it, they can if they put there heart to it, but there heart is not in it. Something came along that sound good, and maybe there are depressed and broke at the moment and need something to hold on to. Well my friend if that's the case what you really need is Jesus. That's the whole truth of your situation and that's real. Actually you going to need him whether you in our out (smile) why give yourself one more problem if you are not ready.

You HEAR THAT! I LOVE WHAT I'M DOING! That's simple mean I have a passion for what I believe. You can only be strong if you have a PASSION! For what you are doing other wise you want make it. If you are doing it just for the money you want make it, in business or any other business. Because your desire for building a STRONG FOUNDATION want last if you don't make money and fast. Understanding that everything takes time, it takes study and knowing what you are doing inside and out. It takes you feeling good about yourself and then the business you are in. If I didn't feel good about the Business of 5 Linx Homebase Business! I would have quit a long time ago, it would have been just something else I started and didn't finish. Why because when I was doing other things all I was thinking about was how fast I could make money. The sad part about the other business was I couldn't make it fast so I didn't last, This business is not about making it fast sure, we want to make money and going to make money. We can make it fast or slow in this business [BUT] THERE'S THAT WORD [BUT] You have to understand the concept of money and Business it's more than just about you!

This Business of 5 Linx Home Base Business, this is the first thing they teach us about Business. Who are you helping? If you are not helping no one then you are in the wrong Business. This business is built where we have to help one another if you plan on making it BIG! In this business and that what I like about it.

Don't get me wrong I don't want to sound like a fake brother, trying to make you think I don't want to make money. If making money is not important to me, that's the furthers from the truth I want to make money, and a lot of it. I SAID I WANT TO MAKE MONEY! YA HERD? NOT MONEY MAKING ME! So with this attitude and a Strong desire I can You Can make it. Like I said at the top only the STRONG SURVIVE!

You have to want to help some body, and can't be all about you and your bling, bling.

Being strong is what keep you in the game a strong mind, a strong why! is even better! Why I need to do this is what going to keep in you in the game of success. Having to believe that you are willing and able to do this. I am willing to build a strong foundation, that can't be rocked by no one. You have to be strong enough to say to your self and other I am going to do this thing so get the HELL! Out of my way. You have to be strong enough to wither the storm. To bounce back up when you fall, if you fall a 100 times then you get back up 101. With your determination now stronger than ever, remember Popeye the sailor. When he got tired of being knock down he ate his spinach and came back stronger.

That what we have to do is every time something come our way, our spinach will be Jesus (oh Lord)! And get back in the game remember one thing you called the game the game didn't call you. It was your desire to make it, you said you want it now here it is. Or you a man or mouse, don't let nothing or no one get in your way of success.

When people don't understand your dreams or thoughts, they will say negative things. So don't talk to them about your dreams are what you are doing, once you see they don't understand. They will just make you weak in start giving you 2ⁿᵈ thoughts, the next thing you know you will be out of the game.

In the 5 Link Business, we all are leader and that's great. But still we have to have an appointed one sort of speak to lead a meeting here and there. That's where my partner and I come in DW. When leading people you see a lot of different attitudes. Some strong and some weak, now the weak ones I tell you they are hard to deal with. But I have to show love to all of them, but here's the deal I said it one time if not a 100 x that.

Business like this or any other business you are not going to make money over night. It's a building process.

1. You have to start with you, we have to re program you. Why because you been doing things the same old way for 15, 20. 30 years. You have been train to make money one way, that's hitting BOSS CLOCK!
2. You have to understand the New Business You got in to.
3. You have to learn how to present the Business, how can you know it, if you don't know it
4. You have to build a reputation not only for the Business, but for you. people don't know you for doing business. They know you from the factory work, store etc.
5. Most of all you have to nourish the Business you just discovered, it's you baby, you have to handle it with care, you have to be willing to watch it grow. You have to sometime go out and cut off the bad braches sort of speak to help it group up! But if you are not willing to wait and watch, you want make it. If you are strong enough to go ahead when other go the other way you'll make it. If you not strong enough to take the hits of life you want make it.

But if you are strong enough to take the hits, if you are strong enough to get back in the ring no matter what. If you can get a black eye and then think to your self that all you got, then you better watch out. Because I'm tired of being tired.

I'm tired of some one else running my life, I'm tired of my family being in poverty. Say too your self, I WASN'T RESPONSIBLE FOR THE WAY, I CAME IN THIS WORLD, BUT I'M SURELY RESPONSIBLE FOR THE WAY I LEAVE.

AND NOT ONLY THAT I'M RESPONSIBLE
FOR OTHERS I LEAVE BEHIND.
ONLY THE STRONG SURVIVE!

CHAPTER IV

BEING SETTLED!

Jan 06, 2014

Are you one of those people that have in your mind, that you have a good job! You don't need another income. You're all right! As the youngster said, well that good if you are still in the 19th / 20th century.

Yes coming up in the Good Old Days, yes there wert plenty of jobs. So we were taught to finish school go to college, get a job at a good corporation work 30, 40 years get your platinum gold watch and retired and live happily ever after.

I HEARD LESS BROWN SAY, FINISH SCHOOL GET A GOOD JOB! RAISE A FAMILY AND DIE! BASICALLY THAT'S ALL YOUR DONE!

JUST OFF THE PRESS! PLEASE READ THE MEMO! THOSE DAY ARE GONE!

People that are finishing college can barely fine the job they went there fore. Here's the deal once upon a time, only the white were going to college mostly. Blacks were not allowed in most cases. So they fore they had high paying jobs they were plentiful.

Just a little straight talk here, just being 100! If I don't tell the truth no need of me trying to write a book ok! Back in the day the white people

CHAPTER V

POSITIONS & CONDITIONING YOURSELF

JAN 06, 2014

This chapter is all about being in the right place and taking advantage of it. You hear people talk in church about being in the right place for your blessing. I believe in Business can be the same way, it's about being in the right place. Being in the right position and knowing how to condition your self to stay there. It all about attitude of where you want to be in life. You know many of opportunity have come and gone. For some reason are another we didn't get in on the ground floor so we miss out. Either we didn't have the money are the mind set. Meaning we didn't believe are we thought we were all right again there's that word [all right]. I remember Les Brown asking a group of people, would they like to live comfortable? They replied yes! He then told them in order for them to do this they need to be rich.

We have to come to the reality of one things as long we are working for some one else, and depending on that one income you are not all right. The old man I talk about in the last chapter depend on one thing all of his life and that was his job being there day after day for close to forty years. Once upon a time that might have meant something to the owners. but there that word again [BUT] the owners sold out to a corporations and these guys wasn't close to the workers didn't know and didn't care.

There bottom line was the $ bills, if you wasn't making them you wasn't staying. The name became numbers and that's what you were a number, that's what I was a number. Go into the office for any reason they ask you your number. I quite sure some where in his life he had a chance to try making money some where else. Great opportunity like Excel, PC, Google, one local like Wal-Mart, when its was coming up. No average person saw the big picture. No average person that was making a little money saw the reason to position and condition there self to what was coming.

And before you know it in there life time there became millions airs out of there investment. The smart people took a chance to make something big happen for them and there family. They position there self for this and condition there self to stay above the haters. I believe the smarter people in the world don't go out and ask question when some thing great come along. Instead they act on instinct, they move on gut feeling. I all ways said act on what come first, if you feel it do it! If you question it you loose it! It's just that simple.

People are so afraid of trying something new, that they will come up with any excuse not to invest in there future. I know an old man now still talk about when he could have invested in Wal-Mart for about $1,500, said he had the money and was about to invest with so more fellows on the job. But they let one guy talk all of them out of it and to this day he still crying about the mistake he made. 45 years plus later he still talk about the money he could have now if he hadn't not listen to one guy, that didn't have a clue. The one guy that didn't understand the possibilities, of what that little more could have grown into. He was wise enough to in vest, but he was just smart of enough to stop other from there dreams. There are people out there that can do that, if you let them. It's best to keep your thoughts to your self. There are people are jealous of you! And they don't know why, they just are!

People that become millions airs, are people that live off of there gut feeling. Not afraid to loose to win. You hear what I just said, you have to loose to win sometimes. Position & Condition yourself to take the bitter with the sweet. Either, you are going to coming out great.

Because you know the chance you are taking and your not scared, remember the old song SCARED MAN CAN'T GAMBLE, A JEALOUS MAN CAN'T WORK

It's true

If the thought of you loosing money scared you to death, don't gamble! Put keep in mind if you are working for some one else you are taking a risk any way! How you ask.

The job may shut down, you may get fired, you may get hurt, you may get sick, you may never get that raise should I go on. Job are not loner the way the use to be, some times the need for people are not like they use to be. The love for the human man the worker is not like the use to be. I remember the time when a man got fired, and we felt like he was fired for no good reason. You could talk about it and possible get his job back. But now they don't need a reason to fire you, and don't have to give you no reasons. I have worked both of these types of job, really still to this day, I wouldn't want to work a no union job! And they are hard to find these days.

I'll tell any one when a great opportunity knock you need to answer. Quickly, respond quickly, act quickly. Why? Because it might just pass you by. Here's the deal.

Opportunity never stop knocking, but it will pass you by, and that you let pass you by some one else will see coming. And they will take advantage.

See while you teasing your self, talking about let me google it. And let me think about it you are loosing out on a great opportunity, possible the opportunity of a life time. Great opportunity are only great when you take advantage of them. People these days that are scared to act on things, that you might show them about. They are quick to say let me Google it, that's find that there right, but I know they are not going to Google any thing, or check in to nothing I know this. But what they will do is go and tell some person, about this business that neither know anything about. One broke person will tell the other it's not going to work, and that person will very easily believe that broke as you are person and there it is. You will never change. Broke people shouldn't ask broke people in 99% of the time for advise.

Change calls for action, call for faith, and for you to be able to think out side the box. Being able to allow you mind to stretch, and again you have being program and tagged to work for some one else. These people don't want to loose you, because you are taking care of them too good.

They have programmed you to think that they are taking care of you! On the real you are, I have taken care of them for years.

It's almost like legal slavery! But now they give you a little money and can stop it when they get ready. Why is it a man can worked for years driving a used car. As soon as he buy a brand new one, every one in the office are on the line is talking. You can't even drive your new car to work scared you are going to be fired or harass, it's sad. I remember on the job back in the day, the white superviser bought a new used car it looked good true enough. Look like everyone wanted to see his new used car! Said good things about the hold nine yards. Brother went out and bought a new off the show room floor car, talked about it had 1 no miles on it.

Only a few people went out to see it, the others said he was going to lose it. Some say he was selling drugs the whole nine. No one stop to think what ever he was doing he have a note he has to pay it wasn't cash. So there a chance it was hard work and good credit. I just threw that in for free. But that's just the way the human mind have been program. That the way it is but can change it if you like.

But now you have the opportunity to have freedom in you life but you are scared. Why because Massive have showed you the clock for so long, you can hit it with your eyes close, he like that. Doing it with your eyes close, you have did the same work day after day and now you can do it with your eyes closed. You have even got so use to making the same money week after week, month after month, year after years decade after decade. Now you can open your check with your eyes close and know what in it. The same money.

But your so scared of chain if some one even talk to you about some thing new that going to great for you and your family, your cuz then out and tell them to move on. You'll tell them you got a good job and they love you. Ya! Part of that right they love the way you help make them make money.

You know as I think back from the 1ˢᵗ job I ever had to date, for some reason I all ways got in trouble. Never could figure it out It wasn't like I was just looking for trouble but trouble seem to fine me. It wasn't until latter on in life when I figure it out and the answer was simple, I didn't like working for no one else. I all ways wanted to be my own boss, I had big dream that faded away too. I wanted the best of life with people waiting on me not waiting on people.

I worked jobs for long period of time by the grace of God. But I hated every minute of it. My dream was as big as the next fellow. My problem was just as many are today not knowing really how to get to the next level. But I had to do something I had to learn how to position and condition myself for a new way of life.

I knew I was getting older and one day I was going to have to retire, just to go back to work. This is the very reason when I, saw a great opportunity I took it. I knew the rate I was going I was going to me the one retired with nothing but a small check with a bunch of bills. Possible a new job application in my hand on my way back to work. People around me would talking about retiring, but the thought just scared me, the reality would never seek in. I know one day if the Lord Bless me to see that day I would have to. that's ok I'm not scaring of retiring itself I deserve that. People as a hold deserve that.

But what I don't deserve all of my life, retiring and going back to work that what scares the hell out of me. I see it happen to often, I know an older lady that had just retired. She was in pretty good shape as far as I could see health wise. She told me Jody I'm going to retire and just sat around and do nothing.

I even was the speaker at her surprise retirement party. We had a nice time and she spoke and told the people the same thing she had told me.

But some how in her voice I knew she would be back in the work field in less than a year. It was about six months later she was looking for part time work. Man this is scary and people wonder why I all ways trying something new to make money. I'm just crazy enough to believe that one day something will happen BIG! If I keep trying but if not I will never know.

CONDITION & POSITIONS HIS SELF FOR THE FUTURE.

CHAPTER VI

HAVING FAITH

JAN 06TH 2014

I just like to talk a little about having faith in God, Matthew 6:33 tell us :33 But seek he first the kingdom of God and his righteousness, and all these things shall be added unto you

I believe this from the bottom to the top of my heart, there fore it's not hard for me to believe the thing that are un seem to the human eye

It have been said that "science says "SHOW ME & ILL BELIEVE "FAITH SAYS BELIEVE & I'll SHOW YOU"

That's the different in God and man, man can only want you believe after you see. But God want us believe and did see his word come true, so what do you want to believe. I see church folks believers and none believers having little faith, they talk a good game, but when it come down to it such little faith.

You want to start a Business you feel that it's the thing for you, you even feel good about it. The little faith that you have you let some one discourage you, "SHAME" on you. Let me tell you something, don't let know one tell you, you can't do something. People are so quick to tell some one else what they can't do, or what want work and have never tried it for them selves.

Some thing you have to keep to your self especially if you are weak minded. The lord put something on your mind to make life better for you and you go run tell some one else. Testifying in church what the Lord have told you to do, and then here come the devil bringing you doubt about what said the Lord. Now you don't do it because you been trick by the devil, that playing to be your friend. See that person saw threw your blessing and thought you might get ahead in life. Now you may never know, and that same person will be telling some else huh! He/she God told her to do something and they didn't do.

Know all the time that person allowed you to step in the way of a blessing. That's the way life is you have to be careful. When you pray for something and ask for a break threw and it come, at least have the faith to walk out on it. Know what the end is going to be. How because you follow what was laid out for you. It's your faith that made thing possible for your life to change.

Keeping the faith in what ever you do can bring about a change, action brings about a change nothing change on its on.

You have to have faith in your self, it's very important. The way you talk, walk, think. This can send a postive vibe to the person you are talking too. This will let the person know that you have a strong believeth in you and what you are doing.

You know in the Bible where they talk about walking by faith not by site, this what I'm talking about by faith we can do the impossible, by faith lives can be change, your way of thinking and living can be change. When you learn to have faith and believe in you. You when you sale you to you, then you want have problem making a sale to no one else.

People want things that they are afraid to go after, so what if it don't happen this time then try it again and again if you have too. Who said it have to happen the first or second time any way who told you that. There are many successful people will tell you that they may have tried business are invention hundreds and hundreds of time. Some where trying to one thing and ended up with something else that made them famous, just manage to stumble up on success from trying something to make something else happen.

It was there belief in faith that they could do it that cause there success to come full circle. You have to do the same thing don't give up maybe it didn't happen like you expect, or as soon as you expect. Have the faith in believing that if you are still breathing you have another chance to make it happen. How bad do you want it! DO YOU WANT IT AS BAD AS YOU WANT TO BREATH!

Now that's serious and that how serious and that's how serious you should be. that's how important it should be to you. It's your life are you tired yet of not having a life style. Some people are just happy where they are in life no matter where they are why? Many different reason, I can't explain but I can, but I want some people just discus me so I want go there. But if you are this far in this book you are not one them. Hear what I said you are not one of them!!

You are a special breed like my self you want and you cant settle for a easy life. It's your guts in side of you that want more, I have no ideal why I'm this way because I never really had any thing.

Everything I ever had that cost anything was used, some one had it before I did. I never ever really been any where to have fun, I never really had a lot of money to spend and just enjoy life like other people do. Even some of my brother and sister bottom line I never had nothing that amount to anything.

Now I do why, I'm tired of being tired and of being the black ball in the family I, want my own freedom. I want a vacation, I want to have money to spend freely, I want to be able to donate to a charity of my choice, look at tv and see kids that need help send money to support and go and see how they are doing. To drive Brand New Car, to live in a house that no one have never stayed in just built for me and my family. Hell Ya! This is what I want and I can't get it unless I believe, you can't get it unless you believe.

No one is going to give it to me and I know this, they will let you see how they are living. They leave you wishing you had this and send you home broken hearted. You have to make things happen for you In life no matter the cost are the embarrassments some time.

Man I have failed so many times in life its not funny! Yes there was time I would just say for get it! I would just be an old average Joe! Go to work raise a family and just die. Haven't enjoyed life at all, going threw life broke.

But then I realize if I go through life broke and the kids and grand kids see me this way, I'm sating a pattern a curse sort of speak of poverty. Some one have to break the chain in this case it's going to have to be me. I have one little grandson Eithan, he just love his papa to death. He talks about being with me all the time and going where I go and doing what I do. So there fore I must be an example to him and the other 15 grandkids. They must at least see me trying to make a different not following a trail but making one for them to follow this is a must.

So if I'm not around one day, they will know what to do or at least take up where I left off. The curse of poverty have to broken some where down the line, other have broke it and I will to trust me as I trust the Lord.

We see successful people every day, and we asked ourselves why cant I be like that.

Why can't I do that and you all ready know the answers to your question.

Because you want take the time out, to take the time out to get your life in order. To do what it takes to make a change in your life. This is why your patients want let you have what your mind desires, because you don't have none. No patients to fight, no fight no gain, you have to settle your self down and get ready for the long ride to success. Some people ya! Its come easy don't hate just look at them as say God Bless them I know minds is on the way. One thing about it if you waited as long as I waited you will appreciate it when it happen.

See we are just a like and there something in side that want let us quit, that's why you keep reading, that why I read and listening to tapes of successful people this why I pay attention to these peoples more in anything this is why I pray and keep the faith. I'm on a mission and it's not impossible. Every man, woman should leave a legacy what will your be? Mind would have to be he tried until he made it, didn't know how to quit, because it wasn't in me! There was all ways work to do some one had to break the chain. Few in the family think they have broke the chains, but not so. It not all about doing for you it about being your brothers keeper.

See when one sibling get out of the box you think, they would try and help the next. Not in this family one get out, in so many words they tell you to figure out like he / she did. I have one brother I tell you he's all about his self. Doing pretty good for his self and family. That's good but what bad he not going to look back and help you with one dime, At least not me. That's not Godly, But {BUT} there's that word again. My daddy I ways taught me you can't be mad about another man money have your own. So that what I'm working on, I just all ways prayed that in the mist of trying to make it I never had to ask this cat for one dime and so far so good.

Notice I get a little side tracked some times, just like my dad I guess I like to say what on my mind. It just a way to let you know the road to success is not all way easy. Its going to first of all deal with your faith, then it will take a lot of pushing and pulling. To make it to the top, but we can do it. It's in us all if we want to make it happen you can. See many have done it before you got here the wheel of success is moving forward.

See you didn't have to invent it, all you have to do is get on it and take the ride in to the your BRIGHT NEW FUTURE. FAITH IS IN YOU!

CHAPTER VII

TALENT & SKILL

Even though there is greatness in all of us, there is a different in Talent & skills. Some people just have nature talent, and some have to work hard for it. I'm one of the guys that have to work hard for it. But that just give me the opportunity to challenge my self and I don't mind because I'm all ways up for a good challenge.

This is where skills come into play, see skills come from hard work. This come from developing yourself in what you believe.

This give you the opportunity to become ahead of the rest, because you are developing your self, or forming your self in to your greatness. Yes it can be hard but easy it what you got you in the situation we are in today. Depending on some one else to chose our destiny. You might think to your self that you are in control, but really your not. You can't even control the money you make every week etc.

You don't really have control on where you can spend your money. What you say? Well you don't say you want to go to the mall and meet one of your kids at 2:00 pm but your job say you have to be there at 2:30 pm. Now what are you going to do? Are you going to be at work at 2:30 are will you be at the mall calling and tell your boss a lie about why you are late!

Either way you still had to be there whether you made it or not, why because you don't own your destiny, you are not in control. You are program to do what that job tell you to do.

But you are ones of the ones that want freedom. You are the one that stand out in the crowd and you know it. You have a combination that is awesome, it's call talent and skill and you want to break the chain that is holding you down. You really want to be your own boss because you are feed up, with what's going on in your life.

I know breaking away is not easy remember what we are, we are humans robots. We are design to do and work for others from a young life. We watch our dads and moms go out to work our grandparents go out to work and retire and die broke.

Now we are taught to grow up and finish school, go to college get a cooperation job. Work there 35/40 years and retire and go back to work and then die. Going the college part is great, wish I had stayed in. if noting else I would be like most people still paying the students loans.

But every once in a while a great opportunity come our way, that allows us to use our talent & skills, our minds to work toward our future, the sad part about this is that we are so mess up some times, are lives are not important. We have been trained to work for some one else. Some will still tell you it's job security. What scfi. Movie they watching.

Some people have one are the others talents or gifts, some have both. But learn to use what God have given you and move forward. when a great opportunity come your way run don't walk towards it. It may never come again!

CHAPTER VIII

CHOICES

JAN.08 2014

Life is full of them from the time you wake up in the morning, until the time you go back to bed at night. This is why you have a mind, because there choices or options you have to deal with every day. When you wake in the morning and see the new day the Lord have Bless you to see it start right there. Do I get up right now or lay here a little longer. What do I want for breadfast? Or do I even want any breadfast this morning? What do I ware this morning, how do I fix my hair etc. etc.

You see where I'm coming from now? This is why they say a mind is a terrible thing to waste. Because of the many, many times in a day we have to make choices to make thing happen for you. Now those are the simple choices and we all wish that life was just that simple and we would go about our la, la, day so easy.

But [but] there's that word again but! It's because of life we have to make a choice to live are just be here. To have a life style or just a life, life style Is having what you want when you want. The choice of deciding that this is my life and I'm going to live it to the fullest. I'm going to work my jelly to make my life great, I'm not going to be scared to try what seem to be impossible. Just because the people in my family and around me couldn't do it, that's not me that's them. I can do the impossible because the word impossible to me just mean challenge! And I'm up for it so bring it on.

Only one are 2 things can happen here, it will kill me are I will kill it. But I'm geared up and ready for the fight.

This is the wise choice and the best choice you can have to conquer anything in life. There are people out there that really want more out of life than they are given. I believe you are one of them, you have to make the wise choice of making it to the next level. Or you can make the choice of just settling and life will give you what's left over. At some point in life you should be tired of getting what just left over are used. The home you stay in used! The car you bought used! Even some of the clothes you wear used!

Just think how good it will feel if you make the choice to succeed in life. The home you buy, you have built from the ground. You are the first one to stay in it, it's brand new it's new and it's yours. The car in the drive way you bought brand new, its' just the way you want the color you want the whole nine yard, it's brand new you can smell the new car smell in it instead of the old car smell.

If just a big different when you are in control of your life, but it just don't come naturally. You have to decide to make a different in your life, and when you make that choice you have to make promise to your self to stay with your wise choice.

Only then will you have a life style, I said before! And I will say it a hundred more times if I need to. We didn't have a choice of the way we come in to this world. broke or with a silver spoon in you mouth. But you do have a choice of the way you leave.

It's your choice of what you do in your life while you are here on God earth. If you make it to heaven thing will be lovely. But if you don't {but} there's that word again. But if you don't why in the hell would you want to go threw hell twice. Hell on earth and more hell in hell. Lord give me a break some where, on the real. Life can be wonderful or it can be a living hell. See after seeing our parent struggle to take care of us, and the people around us struggling trying to make it from one day to another. We need to open our eyes and our mind and say to our selves what do I, need to do, to make my life better and the people around me life better.

It's hard yes it's hard some times and some harder than others. But you have to make the choice to survive. Life can be horrible at time believe me I know, but I made the choice as long as I have breath in my body. And every day that the Lord allow me to see another day I will use it wisely, I will try to make some thing great happen in my day and in my life.

When my days down here are over, and I have to go home to be with my Lord. He will look at me and say well done and smile, well done Jody my son I see you worked hard. You didn't leave your family in debt. And then and only then I will more than sure that I made some the right choice lol!

CHAPTER IX

WHY ARE PEOPLE SCARED OF SUCCESS

JAN. 08 2014

People every where want the good things in life, but they are afraid of the mountain they have to climb. They are afraid they might fail, are scared if I don't make it what will people say. Well here's the deal they will say the same thing about you if you make it or not. See people love to talk and they are going to talk about you any way. Here's the different if you are broke and can't help them, they talk about you in your face. If you have money and can help them they talk about you behind your back.

It's sad but it's true, so it's really doesn't matter either or, success some times come by failure. It's the failure some time that make success so wonderful, it's make you stronger.

Here's the deal every time you fall it doesn't mean you get hurt, it just like walking down the side walk and you stumble and fall. You may look around quickly to see who's looking and hurry and get back up. The fall didn't hurt, it was the fact that you fell and some one might have saw you (smile) but you quickly got back up and went about your way. Because the fall didn't hurt it was the surprise of the fall and who may have seen it, that bother you the most.

Going into your own business are trying to be successful can be the same way when you think you fail.

Here's the deal you spent a lot of time talking about going into business for your self. You talked about it to every one around you, because you were excited and you should have been. That's good you should be excited! If you don't show no excitement then who's going to be excited about what you are doing.

Now the big day come the big opening, you did everything right, you are on your way to the top. The family behind you, your friends are there this is the big day and it don't go the way you plan. Might of fact nothing went the way you plan or saw it. You have just walk upon the crack in the side walk and you fail down.

Now you sat in the pity party, family telling you it's going to be all right, friends smile and tell each other they knew you couldn't make it happen, but they walk up to you and tell you it's going to be all right with a back stabbing grind on there face. Saw you didn't make any money but they want there's. You feel so bad now you just want to go in a corner and die. I know how you feel, I felt that way one time.

I remember when I started to work at this community radio station in Little Rock, Ark.

I did a Gospel Show on this station called KABF 88.3 Fm. Here I did a Gospel Program on a program I now call the Luv Train. I threw that in free lol!

Doing to the fact that we were a community radio station, we didn't get no respect with the commerical raddio station. I notice when I got to the station we didn't get the attention that the other so call big name station got.

But{but} I was just dumb enough to step out, because I wanted to be known in the business no matter what station I worked for. I was from the streets sort of speak and I was going to get what was do for me and the

stay on the radio and that would be enough for me. Here I am 34 /35 years old and I feel like a 7 years kids I was threw with that part. These were church folks and these folks really made me feel bad. So bad for a moment as I walked back to my car I just felt like a kid man I wanted to cry. Thinking this is a mean, mean, mean world.

But before I made it to my car I started to laugh myself at my self. Thinking you a thang fool if you let this mess get you down you are bigger and tougher than that. That when I was able to pull myself up and took it as a learning experience. When you are able to make fun of your self. Then and only then you can laugh with the ones that are laughing at you. So right at that moment that took the fear out of me, now I loved the ideal more than ever of being the worship leaders at program 15/ 1500 + it don't matter I'm the Hug-Man Jody "Gimme A Hug" Luv from KABF 88.3 Fm the Luv Train wow!! Nothing to fear but fear it self.

See what I'm saying I fell down, but it only hurt because 1500 people saw me do it. It wounded me sort of speak for a moment but it didn't kill me. May be that where they mess up because now I'm here and stronger than ever, it was just a bump in the road and the bump was just a lesson that's all. It wasn't about me giving up it was about me getting better.

So when you decide to open a business are what ever you decide, to make your life better to take control of you life keep in mind the bumps are coming. The cracks in the side walk no matter how careful are there. You will fall and it might hurt but get back up, there bigger and better awaits you don't be scared to reach after your dream it's your dream God gave it to you. You have to do it are take it to your grave, no matter what it is can't nobody do it like you. It might be done another way but God have a way he wanted it done by you. Don't let it die in you but let it live with you.

DON'T BE SCARED OF SUCCESS! ESPECIALLY IF YOU KNOW YOU WANT IT!

Just think if I had gave up that night, just because I looked and felt like a fool. So what the fact that I went was great all my itself. There were others at the stations that have been there for years that wouldn't step out. Even though we were community radio stations we had more covered than the so called big stations around town.

In short if yo have the power find away to use it and take advantage of it. Meaning you are a smart and blessed person and gifted at that. Just because you don't shine the way the others do, that don't mean you cant shine. But in order to shine you must step out and be heard, even if you are missed understood are don't speak clear. So one is going to ask what he /she say and who is that. IT'S YOUR LIFE YOUR DREAM CAN'T NO ONE DO IT LIKE YOU!

CHAPTER X

LOOKING OUT FOR YOU

Jan. 8th 2014

April ham Lincoln says good thing come to those that waits, and it also been said only the things left over from those that hustle. You have to realize something and that is everyday you live you are dieing in other words time is running out. You can't keep Putting off your dreams you plan for life. Because when you do this your dreams, ideals plans just start to fade. As you get weaker and weaker on your ability to make some great happen in your life.

Time is like kryptonite in most cases it, if you are not working your plan time is just making you weaker. And before you know it you are dead in your track, your dream just went down the drain. For years I talked about a book I wrote that I didn't never publish. But I talked about so much that people were ready to buy it any they wanted to know where it was it.

After awhile of not getting the book publish, when I got to talking about it no one wanted to her nothing about my poor little book. They would just say let me know when it's out! Ok! Well I knew that spirit it was ya! right you got a book Show to me ok. People get tired of you talking about what you going to do.

What I'm trying to tell yo to quit talking about it and be about your dream, do something to make it happen do more than just talk about it put it in to action. When people see you are trying there are people out there that will help in some cases, and if not don't let that worry you it's your baby! It's your dream so work IT. No doubts life is full of up & downs, disappointments with an (s). But you have to know it not about the knock down because they are coming from family, friends, strangers, just life in general. But you have to be strong enough to get up, if you waiting on some one to pull you up you'll be there a while. Remember its about you and the time you invest in your self, what you believe about you can you do, its easy to say yes! But can you really do it, can you stands the punches that life throw at you? When it look like its over can you find a small hole, crack to come threw to start again.

See when people really want to win, come successful in what they do they don't quit. They hang on for dear life they act as though what they are doing there life depends on it why! Cause it do! What you do better for your life today make for a better tomorrow, you have to believe that. When you are focus on doing better becoming a better you, you will become a better person in society. It's call a "GOOD LOOKING OUT" Greatness is all around you. Something in side of you is hollering to you 'WE CAN DO BETTER THAN THIS. See deep down inside you know you are not the settling type. And this what I like about you. See you know the only way you can look out for you, you have to look out for you. Then the strength and power you have now give you the ability to look for others.

I know some people say they put others before themselves, some may do and that's the kind of heart they may have and that great. Maybe that's the God In them and that's there choice noting wrong with that.

But I'm a true believers that I can't help others the way I like to help others with out first helping myself. There are things in life I have to get right before I can reach out and help and preach to others. On how to go through the struggle in life, the best way of telling some one this is when yo go threw the struggle and this can make you a good example. I don't want to spend my life telling you about some one else that did it. I WANT TO TELL YOU HOW I DID IT! THAT SEEM MORE CONVINCING YOU THINK!

IT JUST AS THE TITLE SAY LOOKING OUT FOR ME! This way when I talk to people you or old, I will have my own story and then they can relate to me … and then and only then I can say IF I CAN DO IT YOU CAN TOO! Sounds a little better than IF HE/SHE CAN DO IT YOU CAN TOO!!

THINK ABOUT IT!

CHAPTER XI

CHANGE

Jan. 9th 2014

People are all ways talking about change! Here's the deal nothing change my itself! Change cause for action that has to be put in place for anything to happen. It's not a magician thing you can't just wave a warn and bam! There it is you have to do something about the way, you are all ready doing things and stick with it. Time after time we talk about losing weight, you can take all the diet pills you want, work out in the gym run 10 miles a day. But if you don't change your eating habit its not going to work the pounds are not leaving. If you lucky you might tone up, but if you interest was to lose weight it's not going to happen until you also change your eating habit.

See it has been said it's insane to do the same thing, day after day and expect the something different. It's like going to work on the same job! Day after day working the same hours an expecting a different pay. It's not going to happen, now if you get a check that just happen to have more don't smile to hard, believe me cause the next one is going to be short. See if we want better in our life then we have to learn to, a just to doing something different. It called making a change for the better, for your future. Think about your spouse your kids, your grand kids if you are there. There have to be a why in your life to make you want a change. If it nothing but you are just tired of being tired that your why.

We as people are funny we get fed up with our situations some time, and then we want to change the world. Na, Na, make it easy on your self right now just change you and then you have a better chance on reaching out and changing the world. But it starts with you, the man / lady, boy/ girl in the mirror. You will be better off.

To many time we get mad and want to change but we don't get mad long enough and nothing happen. You know we might get evicted from our homes, cars reposed, don't have enough money to make inns meet, light being turn off, wife leave cause you don't have enough money, and that's just things that happen to me! Lol

But these are just some of the things that can cause people to go over the edge commit suicide. Just one of them for some people and I just list about 6 or more man life is tough so tough that you have to be strong. You have to have a God and a will to live to survive in your life or you want make it bottom line. Life is not a joke some times you have to be careful you have to be willing to change from I can't make it, to know I can, all is need to make a change for the better. You know some time you not only need to change your job, but you need to change your friend.

Get away from broke do nothing people, see all they can do for you is swap sad story. Girl my light got cut off yesterday can you help me, I would but [but] there it is but my car note is 2 months behind I have to hide it over mommy house to keep it. One sad song after another. You have to talk to them wave at them from across the street down the road are something, because you will never do any thing different and your life will never change as long as you hang around some one that is broke as you. For one can't help the other, remember the old saying 'I CAN DO BAD BY MYSELF} and you can it's true.

Change your environment and you will change the way you think, change the way you think and do things, I promise things around you will start to change. Why because you made the first step it was a change. This is where you and things around you start to change. See when you get away from negative do nothing people your life will change. Ask your self what wrong with my life, what am I doing wrong, and what can I do better. See you know you had a dream once a upon a time and you lost it. Got into the wrong job and the wrong crowd.

Now your jobs where is it taking you in the next year are two, I'm not going to say in the next 10 years are so. See that to long to see a change in your job, may be it time for something different! If you ever thought about running your own business this is the time to step out do it now! Why now cause it's time it's been time! I'm not telling you to go in today and tell your boss you quit! That would be foolish get your self position & condition for a move to do that one day soon. Get the knowledge that you need know what you are doing inside out & outside in, be cocky about your self learn how to sale with a smile.

In this business that we are in called 5 Linx Home Base Business, I thought it was one of the greatest thing that come along sense being able to put a phone in your pocket. So when I heard that I could improve my life in a short time, get residual income weekly and monthly, the company give you a BMW & Bentley once you reach a central level in the Business, let you share part of the company profit. I was like where I need to sign why? First of all there was a change and a opportunity to have a life style for me and my family. I saw a chance to take back the life I loan out for years to other people to help build there dreams. Here is a great opportunity to start back on mind. See you mind is like a ball of clay when the clay is soft you can still mold it. but when he gets hard and you try to break off a piece it crumbles up.

In others word while your mind in still in the shape to be stretch, let some new ideals come in and out. Don't be afraid to go after your dreams, you are still a dreamers I know, WOW! Look how far you can in this book sometime we need people to remind us of our dreams.

CHAPTER XII

IMAGING

If you can still imaging something beside of what your doing now, you might not be wounded as bad as you think. You might still have the fight in you to go after your dream & make it come true. Sometime we get so messed up in life and so busy keeping our boss dream alive, that we for get all about we had one. But if yo can still see in the future and believe what you see you will be all right.

It may take a little work on you but there is hope still. You know we are going to have to deprogram you. See the people you work, we worked for, have made us out of robots. Program to do what they have for you and that's it. They even made us think we were making a lot of money by letting us do over time. Which was really an 3 way split, you the Uncle Sam, and the company.

Remember how when you went to a job and you were just going to be there for a little while because, you had a dream to do something better. You were going to go to school and be this big what ever you were going to be. But after being there for a while the dream got smaller and smaller, and when you talked about leaving and getting out of the system to the people that were already made slave to clock they would look at you and laugh, as thought they were saying ya! Right I heard that before. Ya! You know where they heard this from most of them had said the same thing.

If you are young and reading this book take advantage of what I'm trying to relay to you. Your imagination is young and fresh, your mind is like clay that is soft. Soft clay can be molded in to something great don't let that little money fool you. Get out and run as fast as you can. Don't let no one are nothing get in the way of your dream. Even if you not so young like my self, don't give up or given in there noting worth your soul and that's what you will be doing selling out to a lesser life than you can have.

Sometimes we just have to go back and let our imagination run wild, let it take control of you and just feel the freshness that is still left inside of you. I believe that there a place in your mind that have never been touch, it have been preserve just for this moment when you decide you were going to do what you all ways wanted to do.

This is the side of your mind that have never been taped in to by negative people. This side of your mind when you plant a seed, it will not only grow but it will grow tall and wide. I call this the green side and it's fresh and every thing is still possible. If you can imagine it and believe it then is still possible for you to be successful. Don't let nobody walk on your green grass, but you. There should be a sign there saying stay off the grass.

Its fair to say if you can still see threw the smoke, then you are still a dream chaser and that great! Please don't give up on your dream, no one said it was going to be easy. No one said it will come over night. But if you can imagine your dream coming true then it will. I believe in the old saying its better late than never. I rather be a had been than a never been. It least one day I can say I actually tasted freedom for real. As long as you work for some else you are not free, you just have a weekend pass. And sometime you don't get that.

THE TITLE OF THIS CHAPTER IS CALLED IMAGING! See even at my age I'm still looking for that success that I desire so badly. I CAN JUST IMAGAINE MY SELF FINALLY MAKING IT. BEEN INTERVIEWED ON A NATIONAL TALK SHOW OR NEWS PROGRAM.

They bring me out on stage to be interviewed, and they say something like this guy is a over night success,,,, I just wanna be able to say, no I'M A LONG TIME IN THE MAKING … CAUSE I DIDN'T GIVE UP… MMMM IMAGING THAT!

CHAPTER XIII

SACRIFICE TO PARADISE

JAN 10TH 2014

This is really an understatement Sacrifice to Paradise, meaning simple you going to have to first of all give up your old way of thinking. The old way of thinking and making money is not working for you. Now you realize this, the little money that you are making on your job when you think about it really just putting you in debt. By the time you spilt the money you make every week, buying gas, paying bills and trying to eat. Right after you cash your check you need to hurry back to work and try to make some more because that is gone.

What I like about the 5 Linx Home Base Business I got in, is this the mystery of whether it works are not is solved! There is no mystery it's a proven fact that it works, not only that I'm making money and know people making money & doing great. These people have taking control of there life and are helping others like myself to do the same.

That what I love about this Business it seem like every one love every one, why? Because we need each other to get and stay ahead.

So what I'm saying to you the question of whether are not it's possible is out the door. We are pass that point is it possible, yes it is ok! So lets not cross that bridge again. The question is do you want to do what we know is possible? You taking control of your life. Can you man up / women up and take on the challenge to make a different in your life, your family and friend life. Can you step out of the shadows of others of what they did are didn't do.

See we can no longer do the blame factor. We are good as people as doing the blame game. I couldn't make it because mom & dad didn't have the money to send me to college. I could have made it but my friend are some family member mess me up. Get over it, get up off your butt in get in the game. You can side line yourself if you want to and soon you will be in the blenches. You want be good for nothing but watching others succeed.

You have to make a decision to do something about your life your future. Make a short term and long term goal. Sets date and try to make them happen. If you don't make your goal then set another one and try again. The reason why you should write this down.

When you can see where you are going it a better than going at it, just by thinking about it. You have something to go by other wise you will be stuck like a deer in headlight. Even worst like a squirrel in the middle of 2 way traffic and cars are coming, you'll need a split the decision and quick or just lay down and die.

And that's what some people do they just give up and let there dreams die. They don't care no more and just quit, and become a part of the systems of do nothing. Just take the easy road in life, you know the one when you go to work for some one else you don't even have to think no more. Now they have it written down for you, since you couldn't or won't follow your own lead now there's one written out for you. Now keep in mind this is some one else dream some one else business so you don't get paid the big buck they do!

Some of you have been talking about running your own business for a long time, a long, long time. But now is a time of urgency it time to get back in the game like never before. Time is at hand and you should treat it like your life depend on it because it do. See people will only believe In when they see you taking action in doing what you are talking about. It very easy to talk about something and do nothing.

Remember what I told you about the book I never publish, I talked about and some wanted to buy it but I never got it publish. So later own when I talked about it, it was like ya right let me know when you get it publish. In other words they didn't want to hear not one more thing about it until it was in print in stores are some where.

The same thing applies when you talk to people about owing your own business, what ever it might be if you not showing the people something it want interest them for long. Not only that it want interest you long either.

This is the very reason you have to quit talking about, and be about what your talking about. No need to try and talk your self in to something if it's in you it will come out. The plan will come together, but {but} there it is, you have to work the plan it's your plan your vision can't nobody do the way you can. I remember there was a song "No Body Do It Better" if there wasn't there should be lol. Why because if the Lord give you a vision and you don't do it, he will give it to some body who's not scared to walk on water (FAITH) yet and still is not going to be like it was when he told you to do it.

For example when the Lord told Noah, to build the Ark. He told him how he wanted built down to the last nail. If he done any thing different it might have sunk, but Noah believe and did what God command and it worked out perfectly. If he's the God that never change, and I know he is. Then why would I think if God told me to do something are you! He wouldn't lead me or you on how to do it, if there was a question there. The only reason he wouldn't or couldn't lead us is this we never got off the couch. We never lead the project so how can he help us, he help those that help themselves. Just like in the business world crying, all the time want get it. be honest with you it's late in the game for me. I just don't have time for people with tears, I told you before and I will say it again "ONLY THE STRONG SURVIVE" no place in the Business world for cry babies. Unless you are opening a Day Care! Sorry! no I'm not.

Excuses, tears, I can't, I don't know how, and any other thing you think about along this line of disbelieve automatically count you out as a winner in anything.

The doubt that you took with you to your project just killed it, even if you thought it to your self don't let it come out of your mouth. Tell the devil he's a stinky lair andn then go and pray that the Lord see you threw. But you have to be willing to go threw. The storms, the sorry sometime its brings the mountain yo have to sometimes climb. It can be a struggle to the top, but only the strong survive. This is how winners are born, they wither the storm of life and don't give up are look back. No need to look back because there's enough still to come. What's behind you in in the past the present is here and the future is on its way. So look up and be strong and I'll C.U.@. D. TOP!

CHAPTER XIV

IS IT REALLY IMPOSSIBLE?

Jan. 10th 2014

Only if a baseball player refuse to swing the bat, is it impossible for him to hit the ball. If the basketball player refuse to shot the ball in the goal is it impossible for him to hit the point.

The running back that refuse to run the ball is it impossible for him to make a touch down.

But the truth is it's not impossible, they just didn't do it. My point is it's not impossible for you to run a successful business, only thing make it impossible for you is you want do it. It's not if possible to write a book if just start writing. When I started on this book I had no ideal I had so much to talk about, until I started writing.

I didn't worry about how I was going to get it publish, there was no need to worry about that at least until I started writing. So it's possible to make your dream come true but only if you start on your dream...

The late Great Nelson Mandela once said, IT ONLY SEEM IMPOSSIBLE, UNTIL IT'S DONE. So until the baseball player swing the bat, the basketball players shoot the ball, football player run it, it's impossible for any of these guys to succeed. The same for you unless you take a swing at you building your dream it's not going to happen. But once you make up your mind to make it happen to succeed then and only then will opportunity open up for you.

Life is full of choice and the one you make good are bad can be for a life time of happens are destruction. Your decision you make can actually make you are break you it can determined the rest of your life and your kids and generations to follow. To reason why I talk about generations all the time is because it's at stake. Look at Sam Walton and what he did for his family and others like him that went out and went for there dreams. Because of what he did, some other issues may come up. But there will never be an issue of being broke or doing with out, or being hungry in that family are family like his.

I heard some one say I wouldn't want to be that rich, and I'm quite sure he didn't want to be that broke either that why he took control of his life. You know who can say that he saw all of this coming, you can't say that he plan to be this big. But great thing happen to great people with faith to believe you can make a difference.

You might just want a little store in the community that catering to women needs. And before you know it one day you have a store around the world that caterers to women need. You just never know where your efforts and believe might take you. What levels you might reach to be the one that make it for the family. People only talk about not trying to be successful because they are scared to try.

So that's just the easy way out, no one broke is satisfied with being that way unless they are just a fool. I can't believe that and only id you have just given up all hope and then there something inside of you wishing for better.

Just to know that it's possible for me to have my on million dollar business, my dream home, kids have great educations, new cars in my drive way, take a vacations when I want as long as I want, have generations of wealth for my family and to know the will of God that made it all possible is the reason for me to keep reaching for my piece of possible. Possibility is waiting on all of us, the sky is the limit and this is for real, the bounders are limitations that we come across are the one that we put there.

Don't let nobody tell you your dream is not possible, if they do you look at them and ask you lost you will to live or what, you quit dreaming and so you want me too. You know misery love company and they want you as a friend. Ha! Ha! You let them know that it all possible you have to just believe. And if they can't you run, don't walk away from that person. Until he/she gets there thoughts backing and get in the game get away from them. Because they are walking dream killers! The bad part about it there self esteem is so low don't even know what there are doing no more.

What really got me involved in this writing this book, is when I got in the 5 Linx Home Base Business. That my partner D.W. Don White introduce me to, I had just come out of a similar business call FHTM. Which was said to be a scam "aledgally" a scan and a lot of people lost money. I lost some but I, didn't make any.

So when he brought to me I was like so MIGHT OF FACT HELL NO" but once I got in and saw I was making money I was glad to be and still apart of 5 LINX.

So started having meeting the team started to grow and some my God! Didn't have a clue about business.

It amaze me how you can work so hard and so long for some one dream. So long and so hard to make some other family you don't know rich. But {but} there it is but you can't give yourself 1,2,3, years of part time in making your family wealthy.

It's not all your fault it's your up bringing in the way you are trained.

Here's the deal the rich teach there kids how to keep you focus on keeping them rich. Keeping you busy and focus on there dreams, if one try to get out of the system sort of speak jump the fence. He must be the smart one so give him a raise to make him/her feel better about staying a part of the gang.

Then there your family that is use to be told what to do, so they get you use to be told what to do. So here's the deal that work fine with the rich man, so you don't know what to do unless there are direction to do what to do. So you can't start your own business why, because you don't have no direction to read and show you how put together your dream or your dream team. So it all work out for the other guy that have some direction for you and that help keep his dream going.

Leading you to believe again that the possible is not possible for you!

CHAPTER XV

YOUR PAST SHOULDN'T STOP YOUR FUTURE

JAN 11TH 2014

I know there are some that feel they can't make it, because of who they are and what they have done. Who there mom & dad are, may be what there brother are sister may have done. You know society have a funny way of accepting people. You know if you come from a high class family. Dad and mom seem to be doing every thing right and when that child come along you know everyone think the world of them every one expects them to make it. So society will make a way for that child no matter what they are doing good are bad in life hey Mr. so & so kid he's all right, kid bad as hell but because of whom his parent is, are grandparents are, they get a break.

That just the way it is! But here come the kid like me that don't have that type of up bringing sure I had good parents. They taught us well but we didn't have a lot of money etc. so I didn't get the breaks that others did. I was sort of speak a no body in society and for a long time I didn't give a hoot. Doing everything wrong was a bad kid. I barely finish high school but I finish, and got crazy doing the stupid stuff. Going to jail the dumb stuff, smoking weed, snorting before I came to my senses. I just did the dumb oh! You want to know the rest you have to read the other book. I talked about but never publish, it's finally coming.

My point is this I did a lot of wrong, before I came to my senses and got saved. But all the people want to talk about when you try to do something right is what you did wrong. That just the way it is I had to come to my sense and pull myself up and say to myself. Sad to say but it was what I did wrong that is, the cause of me trying to do right today. If I was going to do dumb it was best I did dumb at a young age than wait to an old age to do dumb. They tell me that the worst fool in the world is an old fool.

You know the people that look down on you, in most cases should be looking you straight in the eye. So you can see what there hiding. Here's what I'm saying in a nut shell don't 'DON'T LET YOUR PAST EFFECT YOUR FUTURE"

Use your past as a stepping stone into your future. I have a brother that a preacher and I use to tell him he really can't tell the people nothing really cause you haven't been threw nothing. "IF I WAS CALLED TO PREACH, I COULD PREACH ALL DAY" lol.

I heard it said 'THAT WHEN YOU CHANGE THE WAY YOU LOOK AT THINGS! YOUR LIFE WILL CHANGE" and that is true. I had to look at myself, and think what do you really want out of life. I had to take an inventory inside out about me, and see the world as it was. I had to do an inventory on me, change what was wrong with me. See I can't change the world. But I can change me and then what I have to offer the world are people around me can help change some things at least.

But once I became more comfortable with my self, it was then and only then when I could see clearly. Then I could follow the path of success, then I didn't worry about my pass or what people thought are think of me it was then I stood as a man with pride. And realize that the pass was just what it was, I'm living in the present, looking forward to the future, you can't and I want let you take my past and destroy me.

I think it was Frank Santeria that said, The greatest revenge is massive success.

So there is no need to respond to negative talk about you are to you. I just tell them now. TO WATCH ME! AS I WATCH YOU! WATCH ME! GO TO THE TOP!

HERE YOUR ACTION ARE GREATER THAN WORDS.

See people will try to stop you any way they can, it's up to you to be strong and keep moving forward. Again this is how winners are born, they over come there hurtles and what ever in the way.

I guess what I'm saying to you is this, what people think about you shouldn't matter. It is what you think about you that should. See everyone have a story whether it's good are bad. The past is the past, you either going to better your future are make it worst. We have choices what are your going to do with yours!

CHAPTER XVI

PATIENCE

JUNE 11th 2014

The biggest problem I see when people start there own business, is patience. For some reason we can help other build there dreams for years, but we want it over night.

If it would happen over night then ever one will be rich, and no one would have nobody to work for them. I remember watching the award one night and Eddie Murphy & Michael Jackson were handing out an award. Michael drop the envelope & looked at Eddie as though he was saying pick it up for me.

Eddie told Mike on nation TV, don't look at me I make money just like you do. That what the world would say to each other if every one was rich and it was easy to get that way.

So that's why in most cases it hard but it's possible to make your dream come true. It take a special person to really want to succeed in life, it takes a person that really have a big why! Why! They want this change in there life, and the reason why it don't work for many is because they don't have a strong enough why are patience. Your why and your patience must work together.

In the business of 5 Linx Home Base Business, which is network marketing of course with all type of opportunity that works for you. But just like anything else are business you have to have patience and work on building your dream. There is light at the end of the tunnel in this business, there is treasure at the end of the rainbow. But you have to take time and map out how to get there and stay there successfully. you have to have a plan and work your plan. Short and long term goal are all apart of this.

I see people that come in the business and man they are gunho! In there minds with out even knowing are learning the business they already can do this thing. I don't like to put out the fire in people but I, know if they don't at least learn the basic they are going to fail. The first thing they want to do when it don't happen as quick as they like they want to blame the business are the lead person that brought them into the business. I this case it happen to be me, and there it is I have to hear the pity party some have been in no more that 1 or 2 months and they think now there something wrong with my teaching or the company.

People with patience seem to last longer in anything they do, people with patience are the smart ones. See these people way out there option they think things threw. For instant I'm starting something new, all I ever did was work for some one else. So now I want to do it for my self, they realize it going to take time to get it off the ground and time for it to start making money. The average business takes an average of 5 years it have been said really before you start making money. In most cases especially a small business. There's a lot of hard work and long hours awaits you and still may come up short. But {But} there's that word again the people with patience know this and they deal with it. Why! Because there why is very strong and they are on a mission to be successful not to fail. So they will take the bumpy ride to your journey. I like to call it the never land. The land where it's possible for your dream to come true and where you have built something that will last. You will never have to go back to that bad city of broke again.

But you want to escape you have to have patience, to build a full proof escape plan. People with short patience can't wait attitude don't last long there struggle is much harder. They feel like they have to prove something to some one beside there self, they want to prove that they can do it. There's plenty of time to do that when it's done!

See many people can't be gardeners why, because it take patience you have to make sure the ground is right for what you are planting. Dig holes water the garden every day, pull out the bad weed, prune and so on and so before this plant start to grow. If you don't do these things then there's a good chance they want grow.

Your business is the same way you have to work it daily, spend time & learn what you need to know to keep it going and then some. Have to learn your people and your contact, you have to try to stay ahead of the person that doing the same business you are. There a lot to be considered and done. It really going to take a team to keep and get you going.

And when that fail you become "THE TEAM" why because it's your baby! Your dream you still have to make it happen but do you really have the heart for it. Everyone that says they want there own business they will find out they really don't have the heart for it when It all come down the wire. Wanting and having the patience & the heart to do it can some times make a big different.

If you have been working for some one else for a long time and now you going to step out ship to a new territory can be scary. But you have to look at it when you step on the ship of employment it was scary. But you went to work and you "CONQUER YOUR FEAR" only thing different no is you are in charge.

Patience people are mostly your successful people because the realize the important of patience. I know you hear the statement that Rome wasn't built in a day nor will you business be. Just like a brick layers laying bricks, they can only lay one prick at a time. Just watch them some times how they prepare the brick to be put in place. They do it with skill and perfection. Every brick he/she lay have to be just right, they don't want to take a chance of having to knock the all back down to start over.

To many times of that and they want have job for long, so it take patience for this person to lay it right everything need to be in place, so it want tumble down. The same with you when you are building a business, you have to have patience and every thing must be in place.

Every once in awhile I get a phone call and some one say there are dropping out. The inside of me really want to cry out and say hold on wait a minute. You only been at this 5 or 6 months. Give it a little longer try a little harder to make it happen. But instead I do what really I have to do, but hate it at the same time. You notice the word {but}. I will tell them ok! I understand, I want plead wit them to stay are nothing of this nature why! Because it will be just a waste of time. I will let them just keep on making your Master rich (employer) and one day you will wish had stayed.

Another thing I just don't have time for people, that just want to cry about everything. When things not going there way, there are not doing what they need to do to help themselves. They have just sat around and did nothing all week but watch tv, now they want to play the "BLAME GAME" trying to make it your fault for them not doing nothing for themselves.

I have no tears for these people at all they want but, they want go and get. I just don't have time for ignorance. My time your time is important, this is the only time I have short patience it with dealing with people like this.

CHAPTER XVII

INVESTING IN YOU

Jan. 12th 2014

We spend a lot of out time investing in other folks are things. Time doing for other more than we do ourselves. There come a time we need to just shut down and do nothing for nobody but our selves. Just take a day out of your life, once a week and just spend it on you. You know they say you need some ME! Time and it's that time. One thing people will do is run you to death, then after they get threw with you they have the nerve to tell you, you need to get some rest.

When I think about investing in your self, I have to think about the people that get school and income tax money and just wasted it. Why in most cases they aren't use to a large sum of money but once a year. Mostly that's tax time and when that happen people go out and spend like there is no tomorrow. They go out and buy everything they think they wanted. Clothes, furniture, party, cars etc. The bad part about it is this when they go and make these new bill and then the money is gone the bill is still there. Now you don't have money to pay for the car it seem to all ways be the first to go. Some of the other things you bought then fall in line.

Now you feeling stupid and start to wish you had done this are that. The money is gone so It's to late. You didn't pay none of your bills so you are worst off than you were before you got the money. The only thing the money really help you do was to get further in debt, that you can't seem to get out of. They old saying is fools and money don't mix. Not necessarily calling you a fool, but if you don't think wisely you are foolish.

Let say I can let you in on something I been talking about almost in every chapter.

What say if I can show a way to invest a little money and make a lot. What say if I can show you the money, you wait on all year you can make it every month. You think it would really be nice, if you didn't have to wait on money all year. So when you get the little income tax money you want have to go crazy with it. You will have everything you want at least most of it, so when that money come you can just put it in the bank.

Again I'm going to tell you about an opportunity of a life time, but it want do you any good if you don't take advantage of it now. An opportunity of a life time, have to be taken in the life time of the opportunity. We have to learn to invest in our self, quit being so scary, not thinking about failure and think more about success. Once you realize if some one else have already done it your chances doing it is just as great.

You need to learn to invest in yourself, and believe more when you do so. There have to point in your life where you get rid of the fear and just do it. I hate to sound racist again because Lords know I'm not. But we are the only race of people that are scared to takes chances scared of loosing but can't see that we are loosing all the time.

Why because we want in vest in ourselves which is our future, we are so busy in investing in some one else future that we for get about our own. We don't think we can have these things that others have. We think we can't do it but we are doing it all the time we are dream builders but it just happen to be some ones else.

Now back to your income tax checks are the school money that you waste off with no returns. If you would just take less than $400. And Invest in your self in 5 Linx Home Base Business at least you will know where you money went and with in 30 days if you are willable and teachable this money you will have back in 2x plus. But nothing just happen by chance you have to be willing to invest in you. You can't invest in just wait on a miracle to happen, you have to work on what happen to you. If you work on your dream there's a better chance of your dream coming true. If you don't then don't worry about your future, I'm not a fortune teller but I can tell you it looks dim.

People that have dream that's just what they are, but if you are a dreamer that mean that you are a go getter. You don't mind the mountain are the valleys you are the type of person that can come threw it all. So when you invest in you that gives you what you call pride, the pride in you want fall with out a fight, there is a tiger in you now there a reason for it to come out because your future is at stake.

When you invest in you this is just another way of showing your Greatness, something that we all have but want display, It up to you to invest in you to prove to your self first that you can do it. Do what ever you sat out to do, you know it really don't matter in my opinion how long it take to climb the mountain as long as you climb it.

You sometimes hear older folks say I wish I had done this or that in life, or at least did it different. But there are times when it is to late, when you can't go back and get it right or over.

Life is not mean to you, you just make it disappointing to your self. Because you didn't take time out to invest in your future your dream…Mr. Bum Bum was paying you a little money to make him rich and you felt for it. Knowing you could have done better you held on to his DREAM AND LET YOUR GO!!

THEBOTTOM LINE IS YOU HAVE TO DO WHAT GOOD FOR YOU WHAT MAKE YOU HAPPY! YOU HAVE ONE LIFE, LIVE IT AND HAVE NO SHAME WHEN YOU GET READY TO LEAVE THIS WORLD, HAVE NO REGRETS!!

CHAPTER XVIII

STAYING THE COURSE

JAN. 15, 2014

One thing I'm seeing not only in this business, but in every day life. People seem to only stay focus for a little while. When we find a new ideal or a new way of making money, a new job etc. you love it man this is it I'm going to make this thing happen boy I'm going to make millions. Or the new job you went to. Oh! you just love it your boss is wonderful the money is good and in less than a year you all ready, ready to quite why.

Because if you didn't make the money you thought you were going to make over night, you have lost interest. This is common in most people sad to say, but its true.

For some reason we think that the people we work for, or the network marketing business we got involved in we act like they got there success over night. Far from true a lot of hard work and headache went into getting started. I can't imagine it was a piece of cake it took some work planning and in some cases long hour and lost fo sleep.

But when you are trying to full fill your dreams its take that and some more. Success is about staying on the course staying focus on your dream and desires. When you go to a regular job they might tell you the sky is the limit and then they give you a time card. That should be a red flag right there, when they gave you a time card. That was your first limit there the time card a limit of 40 hours a week unless we say more. Well that along can discourage what you are trying to do, but you took the job so now you need to stay the course.

It's all about giving it your all regardless until you can do better. But it just a good practice to do your best at all times. So we have to finish the way we start that the only way you are going to be great at anything. I know the Business we are in called 5 Linx Home Base Business the sky is the limit. But here's the deal people have been fooled so much they don't know what to believe any more understandable. But if you are interested try it for your self don't miss out on a real good thing because of a bad past get over it.

You know life is crazy it just like a couple of bad love affairs, you thought you had Mr/Mrs right! Boy you went all out for this person and you thought this was that dream person. So you gave them your all and bam! And it was all over, you said you will never love again, but one day you tried it again and the same thing happen so now you are mad at the world and at any relationship that come your way, so you don't rust no one. So now the right one come along and now you have your love shield up, because you are scared of being hurt again.

So now the person that actually love you can't get the love in return. He or she get treated bad because of the way some one did you in the past that have nothing to do with what could be a great future but you are scared. Because everyone you trusted in the past have left you even the dog. So now it hard for you to trust, so you will spend your life in fear.

That's the same way about a great opportuniy some people have been threw so many get rich over night schemes, that when a great deal like 5 Linx come along they are scared to act. And the ones that do they are still so mess up from the last romance they had with the ordeal they can't stay on course. The first little e thing go wrong they hollow, I told you that it was the same as the rest!

The only way you are going to stay in the lane, stay on course is this. For get about your last love affair. Its over it's done the flame is out so let it stay out quit spending your life trying to bring back life to the dead. Let the dead bury the dead! You can't have a future living in the past. That the same way about a great opportunity like 5 Linx Home Base Business. If the other thing you got involved with didn't work great fine let it be don't worry about this. It's a new day don't worry about what didn't work that just a waste of time focus on what will. Stay on the course that going to bring you happynes. See life is to short to worry about things that didn't are want work. If you been threw some bad things in life, and you survived that was just a life lesson you were blessed to learn from that. You know that's a no, no, and now that you are on the right track, the right course you can go forward with your dream and your future all ready look brighter.

CHAPTER XIX

THE ENEMY IN YOU!

Jan. 15th 2014

Think about it some times we can be our worst enemy, the Bible even tell us that death can lie in the tongue. You have the ideal of a life time & your feeling good about, you just know it's going to work with out a doubt. So here we go you go tell girl / boy I thought of this great ideal that can make lots of money put me on the map and road of success. This is what you tell your best friend thinking he or she may be in your corner. They don't have your vision neither do they have a clue of what you are talking about.

So what's the first thing come out of there mouth, it ain't gonna work! [it aint gonna work] should have made you shut up and run right then. Instead you ask the DUMB! QUESTION WHY! Now why are you asking this person why! When you should be asking yourself why did you even tell them about it in the first place.

Now here we go you asked the question and believe it or not they have an answer for you. One they have no meaning are facts but! [but] there it is again, it sound good to them and they are smart enough to make you believe it. Now here you are wondering if what they told you was true, should you pursue your dream or just go back to work. Face it if you give up now, you will never know the truth about your future.

Here's the deal when you come up with these ideals think about it, instead of asking some one are telling someone about it. Ask God did he give it to

you, ask God are you speaking to me. Remember when you were praying for something that could get you out of debt. Something that can help you take care you and your kids better. But since you didn't understand instead of asking for his guidance you talk to some one that didn't have and clue. This is where you find yourself stuck in between I don't know & I don't know. Now you have brought out the enemy in you because you have now brought doubt to the table.

Doubt is a very strong enemy in a weak or confused mind, see when you let words like maybe, I guess. I don't know, well I'll think about "these are just enemy to the business world these are some of the words that cause fear the to the mind. Which cause you to set up an enemy camp against your self. Which is sometime hard to get rid of. Remember the movie sleeping with the enemy, that what you are doing in that case there was some one else in your case it's just you and it's hard to get rid of you.

Freedom awaits you outside of your enemy camp, but you have to go outside the wall. See the enemy in you don't want to see you to do well, you have to believe me. it's the doubt factor that we all have. Once you get pass that you are going to be all right if you stop talking to negative people. People that you are around every day, in most cases don't have a clue about getting out of what they are doing everyday so they are settled and happy so they think. They refuse to use what the Lord have gave them common sense. But you on the other hand you are trying to break away from, broke you want you r own business and yo can have it. But you have to try and circle yourself around business mind people!

CHAPTER XX

LIVE LIFE FULL & DIE EMPTY

JAN. 16TH 2014

I heard this said many time especially when I listen to Less Brown, a great motivational speaker. It didn't register until I heard it a few time and then I understood exactly what he was talking about, then I was like ahh! Most people are just walking around likes zombies, what's even worst program zombies to do something they don't like. There biggest plan In life is just to work for some one else, they go threw life easy but yet expecting a lot. If you are looking for some one else job to make you rich in most cases you are really fooling your self. I know I talk about being rich a lot, and some people find something wrong with that. But you know deep in side who really wouldn't want to be rich Some say money want make you happy, well let me try it and see. I see more smiling faces on people with money than people with out.

Here's the deal as far as I can see it, the Bible tell us to but God first in all things and others things will be added. Now that's telling me on the Spiritual & natural side, so you think about it. See the people that think like that like that are people with out vision. If they have vision are dreams that are scared live them out. That why the title of this chapter is "LIVE FULL & DIE EMPTY" This is not talking about going out party like it's "1999" this is about getting your life in order and going for the gusto! It's your life live it fully you have a dream you pursue it, go after it make it happen. You know to many people worry about what people may say,

about you if you fail. You are not a failure! Because something didn't work out, you only become a failure if you never tried in the first place.

All you have to do now is get back up and try it a different way, see because now you have a better ideal on how it work. Don't laugh when I, tell you this, I'll been trying to get here since I was 16. I'm not sure what went wrong I'm 55 now wow! Even if I failed at a thing I didn't give up people with dreams of making it to the top can't give up at the bottom.

See there is something in side of me that steady wanting more, there something in side of me that want let be just settle for everyday living I want more. You know what you want more, we are one of those people that want more. He have to something that's inside that want let us quit, that wants let us stop because of the bumps in the roads are the crack in the side walk. See people don't understand that special something that we have. I can't explain it some time you can't explain love either but you just know you are in it and it feel good. That's the kind of feeling that we have a love feeling for something better and we want settle for nothing less.

Which cause us to live life to the fullest, get everything out of live that you can. You have a dream go for it no one else see it when you try to explain. Don't feel bad it's your dream they are not going to see it some time. So you have to see your dream threw and when you do they will see it. If you don't they never will so all ways give your all it can be discouraging sometimes but baby that part of life. No one said it will be easy 'BUT IT'S POSSIBLE "I remember when the family get together I, all ways had some bright ideal to make money. If it was trying to write a song that I wanted them to hear are trying to invention something.

In most cases they didn't want to hear what I had to say, they would play like they were interested for a moment and that was it. I smiled and went on trying not to get in my feeling to much. But I knew there would come a day when they all would listen to what I had to say. Because that success that I was all ways talking about would be here now. Because no matter what they thought I kept on, no matter what they believe I believe in me and I knew sooner are later the Lord was going to open & shut that door it's going to happen and I believe that.

That why we have to Live Full & Die empty, don't take your ideal your vision to that other rich place. What I'm talking about now that other rich place? It's the grave yard to many people die with to many dreams and ideals. Ones that they never worked on to scared to try to make it happen. And one day if it's possible you are going to die so sad. Why because deep in side you had a chance to change the way you lived and the way the family you left behind is left living. Your ideals and dreams are now around your death bed looking at you with tears in there eyes. Dreams spoke up and said now you are dying sad to hear, but you have kill us. Ya! Bro./sister, you never gave us the chance to live. All the opportunities you have to bring us to life now look at you.

Can't do nothing can't say nothing, didn't even leave a plan behind so some one with some back bone could do what you wouldn't, let us live. Struggle all your life and all you had to do is let us live. By this time ideals spoke up and was choke up and said, there not much to say cause it about over. But you know I was one of the greatest ideal of all time, but what you do with it. Man we could have been at the top, I could be living on in your name. Just think man there would have people from all around the world thinking about you right now. Remembering how you live your life full and died empty. Bust instead it was just the reverse, man you didn't go for it now look.

I deals and dreams were just standing there just dying beside your death bed. Then another voice spoke up with a smile. Dreams & Ideal asked who are you, he laugh and said you know me they were confused. He then laugh and said here's my card I know it want do you no good now yall are dying, he said with a laugh.

By that time there heard the dying man said that C.W.B.! they replied who! He then laugh again and said I'm CAPTAIN WANNA BEE! I'm the one that put doubts in people like this mind so you can't live. They just talk about making it be never really take the step to go forward in life, they are just wanna be's. I just come from down the hall there was another one just like him, she dead now and so are her dreams. Soon and very soon you guys will be dead too, no way out gotta go now some more people waiting to see me.

Just think about the people at the grave yard that never pursued there dreams, never went after there ideals there dreams. I had a Aunt that died and the funeral really wasn't that sad no more than we were going to miss her. But she had nothing to offer the grave but her body, because she 'LIVED LIFE FULL & DIED EMPTY' she died at the age of 84, she went after her dream at a young age and didn't stop until life its self slowed her down and she was still trying to be on the go then. Full filled her dream was successful work with people and helped people she wasn't selfish with her dreams. I tell she was a go getter and that the way you have to be if you are trying to make it.

You have to be a go getter, no one is going to just put money in your hands you have to go after your dreams to make them happen. You notice I said my aunt was about 84 years old. Seem like people with money live longer, one in most cases they are happier yes they are happy in the sense. They can pay there bills on time, pay them off if they want to. They go on vacations when they get ready and stay as long as they want and don't have to worry about nothing when they get home. This lady have been around the world three times before she left here. Not around the country around the world.

When you live life full and follow your dreams, you can enjoy life to the fullest. When the silent day come you can go in peace, don't have to worry about those others coming to your bed side mad at ya! Because you didn't let them live. We you make that finally journey you can really rest in peace. I have to DECATED THIS CHAPTER TO HER AUNT CHARLENE CAROLDINE because she 'LIVED LIFE FULL & DIED EMPTY "REST IN PEACE LUV YA!

CHAPTER XXI

HUNGRY!

JAN. 19TH 2014

To be successful in anything you have to be hungry, you have to really want it with out a doubt. You can't just think you want it, you to have to really want it. See when people start wanting things for the wrong reason you want last. There have to be a desire a hunger in you for it to work.

It's just like losing weight if you really want to lose weight, you're are going to first figure out what you need to do different to make the weight come off. You'll get you some type of exercise plan and change your eating habit. And the eating habit have to work in with your work schedule. The reason why I say that is really, most people spend more time at work than they do home. Once you get the plan enforced you are going to have to stick with everyday not just some days because in most cases it want work.

You have to have a "WHY" one of the first and most thing you need to have a strong reason why you want to have your own business. This is one of the first thing they teach us in the Business of 5 Linx Home Base Business. Your why can be you first of all and these other reasons 'WHY' you kids, your grand kids, just tired of being tired. What's important enough for you to make you want change your life?

See some people just make believe they want to change so they just go threw the motions of changing just to look good. Just to try to fool themselves & others, some times you can fool people but can never fool

70

your selve. Remember the old saying only a fool can fool themselves. Why would you want to go threw life pretending any way. Just be your self if you want do better, if you don't just keep living miserable.

I believe I told you guys in my introduction why I decide to write this book because Every Tuesday night myself and D.W. do similar on this business that we are in. You know I see some good people that come threw, but there way of thinking is off the wall sometime. When we talk about the business and try to explain it, the people they are gun ho baby I, they can do this. They know ten people they can call right now and make this thing happen,

When I first got in the business this sound good when I heard some body say that. The business is about the number game. So that what I try to get them to hear, but instead all they hear is the money you can make and you can but[but] there's that word again you have to learn the business. No one is going to listen to you when they find out you don't know what you are talking about. See if youwere listening once you got in all needed was 2 more that thought like you and 10 points and BAM! If you did this in your first 30 days,you would get $1000.00. This was just BONUS money to let you know the Business was real. but by not listening not following instruction you didn't make it happen. So they start getting frustrated and confused, now they want to blame me are the business. I guess there was no mirror around in there house.

So here's where the problem start to set in, again that was just bonus money and you had 30, days to do that after you got in if not it wasn't the end of the world. Actually it was the beginning of a new life. But you couldn't see it, you now instead of learning from there mistakes, or mishaps they start fading away. Now here come the true you are you still "HUNGRY" you say ya! But your action are speaking real loud. Now you are not coming to the meeting, your are not on your weekly conference call.

You don't talk to your up line, you are doing noting to help your self but you are blaming ever one else.

See the BLAME GAME "I found out that's you want to fought some one else for your not doing what you suppose to do. So here's what I started to hear I don't understand, your not teaching us a enough. I need to go to another level! I'm thinking you need to learn this level. So people have all kinds of excuses for there reason for not raising up. See some people find away to put there shoes on backward and try to run. And they will fall every time but instead of putting the shoe on right they rather just quit running. The same thing get the same thing, if the people that are making million in the business had to go to meeting, do conference call talk to people time after time. What make you think your journey is going to be any easier.

See now I have got to the point if your hungry, Lords know I'm going to try to help and get you help if you need it. But what I learn to watch for is this what are your hungry for. Peanut butter and jelly sandwich, a quick carry out, or would you like to sat down and enjoy your self with a candle light steak dinner?

I was taught something about the net work marketing business by a sweet couple by the name of Terry & Sandy. They once said we love everybody but [but] there it is but we are only going to work with the one that are working, the ones that are hungry.

These are the people that are not wasting my times and there. See life is just to short for just peanut butter eaters, or takes out, we want the ones that want to sat down for dinner and learn more about what's on there plate if you can under stand where I'm coming from if not. Peanut Butter is in the back!

I thought that was mean when I first heard it, I later realize that these guys had been around a long time. They could spot out the ones that was serious from the one that wanted to waste some time and then play the 'BLAME GAME" there are some that are born with the mind of business, and there are some like myself that had to take up the trade. That's ok! If you are really serous about the trade. You have to have passion and be hungry. I remember back in school I took up auto mechanical as a trade, after being it it for a while being and getting greasy it wasn't for me. So I started to flunk out so when time came I got out and took Radio & TV

Broadcasting and my grades were better. Why because I had a Passion & was Hungry for this and I was good at it.

Same thing about business it all about what you want, what you really want. Can you make this work for you are you willing to go threw the test, because there a test that a wait you. Just no way around it the hungry has to be there, the desire have to be there life is hard enough with out making it harder on your self. If you are hungry you will make it happen no matter how difficult it may be. Just have to take the bitter with the sweet. I heard I believe Winston Church hill say "IF YOU ARE GOING THREW HELL JUST KEEP GOING"

CHAPTER XXII

UNSTOPPABLE

JAN 20TH 1014

If there something that you want to do you have to make it happen. It's your dream you have to make it happen, no matter how hard it may be. It's up to you, you either going to work on your dream or its' s going to fade away. It's your dream no one else know what to do with it, God gave you the vision to make it happen, if he wanted someone else to do it he would have given it to them. Here's the deal lets me a 100 with it. I understand the fear, maybe it's new territory, it's taking you out of your comfort zone. But think about when God gave Moses a vision to take the people out of slavery. He took Moses and Moses along out of his comfort zone, he didn't know the territory either. He made excuses why he couldn't but in his case God didn't want to hear them. So God had reasons why he must go forward.

In short I guess what I'm saying is this God gave you a vision, I know with out a doubt he have a plan for it to be finish. His first plan was to present it to you and see if you were up for the task. He know you are but {but} there it is again in the negative. He want to see if you felt the same way. Can you be like Moses and finally put off the excuses and go for it & be Unstoppable? See we ask God to do thing and show us thing and when this happen the first thing we do is question God! Is that you God! Are you sure that you telling me to do this. The Lord says my sheep shall know my voice. So if you ask the question once he have spoken there might be a problem with the sheep not the master.

I was talking to an elderly lady the other day for instance, I was talking to her about the business. She was asking about the Business of 5 Linx Home Base Business. She had told me she didn't trust no one no more especially about this type of Business. She was telling me how she got burnt in this type of business. Then I told her yes I have gotton burnt before my self a few time. But there something inside of me that want let something like that discourage me to stop. You have to have to unstoppable to really go ahead in life, even though you feel used Ok! Water under the bridge that was past tense, can't do nothing about it.

Keep living! Keep On! Keeping On! Baby. If not you will leave the world the way you come in poor, the only place you will make rich is the grave yard. Then she went on the tell me about the church she went to and she wasn't really getting anything out of it. She said she had been praying for another church home. Wasn't long after that a young man she knew. [she knew] he wasn't a stranger. Saw her and gave her a card and told her he was starting his new minsitery and ask her to stop by. Maybe right then her prayers where answered, she said maybe God answered her prayer but {but} there it is she don't know. God said my sheep shall know my voice. Now you see where she brought in the doubt factor just that quick. <u>MAY BE & BUT!</u>

People you have your own mind and common sense use it, if you are really tired of being tired then you must do something about it. You have been threw a lot and you have settled just because you didn't know what to do. Once when you were young you had the fire in you to turn over the world and then sat it back right, you were unstoppable! As you got older things wasn't going your way, your dream and desire wasn't coming fast enough. You watch tv and people around you, were making money young and old. Now you allow the doubt and the pressure get in your way of being successful.

People are telling you, you can't make it guy/girl like you can't make it. Now it's taking so long and your dream is fading, your vision had become visionless. So now you have just become a C.W.B. Captain Want to Bee! The light in your dream has just about gone out, so now what you do is talk about it every now and then. Do you even realize why you even talk about it at all? It because what you wanted to be was meant for you. Lady & Gentlemen it's still meant for you! Your mind didn't stop thinking, you just stop using it and allowed some one else to take charge. What ever your dream was there's a great chance you can still make it happen. I know you can make something great happen in you life, you have a need a desire to be remarkable. Not only to make some one else remarkable but you! You are some body you are important, your family your kids are important.

Just look at your self In the mirror and smile and say

I'm one important guy I'm so important I'm "UNSTOPPABLE" & you have to believe that because once you do. Noting from this point will or can stop you!you are better than what other think of you. You are better than what you have thought of your self in a long time. You have a mind and it's yours it's time to stop loaning it out for pennies on the dollar. If you are smart enough to keep some one else business going then what make you think you can't keep your own going.

Learn to think about what you are doing right now, how you are making it easy for some one else. And not get really paid what your worth, you can keep a million dollars Business going. But you are only get paid a few thousand something wrong, don't get mad at the guy you look at unless you have a mirror in front of you. You have skill and Talent it been proven, you're doing for some one else while they get richer and you and your family suffer. Now it's about time to get out of the rut you been in for years blow the dust off your brain and use it again. You have to get to the point where your mind is no longer for rent. I'm going to use it my self before some one screw it all up. Keep in mind when you go back and get your dream & vision remember one thing. THE RULES ARE THE SAME!! HARD WORK! I heard some one say and Lord knows it true!

There only one place where success come before work and that's in the dictionary.

CHAPTER XXIII

BE LIKE THE HUNTERS

You may ask your self what hunting have to do with building your dream are being successful. I'm here to tell you a lot, I have never took up hunting but I been around those guys. When there season come around there are hyped up gun ho and ready to go. This is the way you should feel about get ready to start your own business, fired up and ready to go.

What I like about these guys they don't run in the woods and go shooting they prepare themselves for the hunt. Same thing you need to do if you are trying to go in business for your self prepare your self for the good and bad. See the hunter knows the odds of he/she coming out of the woods with and dear. So they are prepared for either are, this way he want give up. You have to be the same way about going in the business the possibility of successes as well as failure. But you have to have passion for what you are doing in case it don't turn out right this time. You can try it again and again if you need to in other words you want give up.

I know guys that live for this moment and noting going to get in there ways. I known guys that took off work when they didn't have the time to do so. This is in there hearts and this is what they live for, they save vacation days for this, sick days for this they are unstoppable when it come to hunting. You have to be the same way when it come to your dream, nothing between heaven and earth should be able to stop you, slow you down but not stop! Like I said before they don't just go out in the wood and starts shooting, they prepare. They get together and go sat up there camp may sure everything is all right, put out feed to make sure the dear are what ever they are trying to trap. Find it to be a good feeding place, week are months before they get there.

These guys do everything possible to make sure every details have been work on to make it a good season. And after all of the preparation there's no guarantee they will come home with one dear. They are willing to take that chance why, because they are doing what they love they're hunters and they have a passion for the game.

If there was not one dear shot the whole week at the camp by nobody, you know what each one of those guys will have a story to tell, about the one they almost got.

They greatness about his ordeal they are willing to try it again next season.

Why because it was so much fun trying they have to keep trying until they get they get that big one. There's something in side of them call desire, pride that want let them give up. When they do tagged the big one that just motivate then even more for the next season. It's like a can of Popeye Spinach, it's strengthen then do want more. That the way yo have to see your success in business, you can't give up if you don't get the big account, or your business don't seem to be going the way you think it should. We all think things could be better no matter how good are bad things are going there all ways room for improvement.

Your season will come but will you be there to accept it. Will you be there in the right place at the right time when the right opportunity come your way. You have to position and condition your self for success. Remember the hunter went out and made plan for something to come there way. You think the dear would be around eating on there prosperity if there was no corn for them to feed off of? No way! not if they found a feeding ground down the road. Same way with success you have to be ready the business normally come to the one that ready to do business. People don't have time for you to get ready when the time is right you have to move on it. Just like some morning when I get up to go to the radio station. It's 4:30 I stop by one of the 24 hours gas station to get coffee it's cold. I need to be warm up and woke up I need some coffee now. Go over to get coffee and there's no coffee, the guy want me to wait. That's not going to happen especially when the guy across the street have some ready. See the game is on the it's call life either you are ready are you are not. There's no in between and there are no excuses. In this game only the strong survive! I heard Less Brown say once what you are hunting is hunting you. You can and will meet up the question is will you be ready for it? Or will it pass you by?

You know life is funny some times we don't get a second chance at things some do and don't. I wouldn't want to take that chance of it coming back around when it's already staring you in the face. It a sad hunt when the hunter had done everything possible to get the big one, he did everything just right. Now right there in front of him there's the big buck 8 points. Man if I get this one I will be the man for the next 4/5 years. Remember you did everything right, now here's your moment of bragging all week long until next season and you still have that bragging rights. Because no one have shot the big one yet.

Man you are feeling so good about this, you not even nerves you got this one in the bag. You are ready to tell the boys to come get this one, now you take the aim in the scope. He to close to miss you see the shot right on side if the head you just know he's going down. He look up he see you your aim in now in the middle of his fore head, he's like a dear in head light he's frozen for a second just long enough for you to get that shot off. It's now are never baby so you squeeze that trigger and you gun jams.

He hears it and run off, it over you want see that one again. What happen he made sure everything was right.

Oops! But he for got to clean his gun, don't let this happen to you. Don't come back with a good story when you could have tagged the Big One! Yes it's a hard breaking moment but he's true to the game so he will be back with a clean gun. That will be his story next season are when every he talk about it. Man I could have got the big one but [but] my gun jam! Ok! Why your gun jam! I guess I didn't clean it!

CHAPTER XXIV

WATERING YOUR DREAMS

Jan 20th 2014

A few time in my book you hear my talk about Less Brown, why because I like this guy. He a great speaker and he know what he's talking about I can relate to this guy pretty good. I didn't go to college wasn't all that smart in school I even remember in the 9th grade they talk about putting me in special ed. I couldn't go in those classes I was I ways talking about these guys all the time for being dumb. To keep any one from knowing they were in special ed. They have there own special bell that would ring in there class about three minutes before the regular bell, so they could beat the other to the hall when the real bell ring. So unless they told no one knew you were in the dumb, dumb class.

I get to school one morning at Horace Man Middle School, my first period teachers sent me to the counselor office said she wanted to talk to me. Ok cool I go the office and there she was waiting on me with a smile. Pull out my report card and very nicely show me how dumb I was. Then she smiled and told me but [but] there it is again. There's help for me and she didn't say special ed! She use some big word that meant the same thing she wanted to put me in the dumb! Dumb! Class I can say that, since she said I was one of them. for what I could see there was no help for these guys, as far as that goes. These guys were eight and nineth grader. They were making paper airplane and throwing blocks at each other. I could do that at home I didn't have to come to school for that.

I asked her are you talking about putting me in the dumb! Dumb! Class? She tried to keep from laughing her self and then said no. I'm just trying to help you learn, I asked what to build block and make paper air plane. Before she could say anything else I was smart enough to bluff her I told her right then just take my name off the row, I wasn't coming back to school. Boy if my mom knew I was skipping school are call myself quitting my butt still be hurting. Buts she said ok Mr. Jones but you are going to have to promise you will do better. And better I did, I didn't find my self no longer talking about these guys, guys I was just one step away myself.

Another thing I like about this guy we both have are had radios shows. I can relate because this is my passion being on the radio, man I Love The Radio. Enough about me. Less talk about your watering your dream lets talk about having patience. You must have to watch your dream come true, I listen many of times when Mr. Brown talked about the different things getting your business going one thing in particular I love to hear about was the, Chinese Bamboo Tree.

This is a tree of course that starts with a small but hard nut, in the North East. Once it is planted into the ground it has to watered and nourish every day. If the seed miss one day been water over it 5 years it will die in the ground. After five years of being watered and nourish it one day break the ground and in 5 weeks the tree grow 90 ft. tall. The question then is asked did the tree take 5 years to grow are 5 week? The answer is 5 years. Because it took five years of watering and being nourish for it to grow.

This was just a great example on how to nourish your business, like we spoke many times in this book. If you are planning to go into business you must plan on a process of making your business happen. Like this tree if you understand the concept of, of what was going on to make sure this tree was nourish and watered from the day they planted the seed and it took over five years to make it grow.

It have all ways been said it takes five year before the traditional business see a real profit. Now I didn't say make money but really see a profit.

I would believe in most cases that would be a small business. But the question is whether you are willing to hold out that long are could you hold out that long for you business to start paying off. This all the depend on the individual I guess, just think if you did hold out and you business grew like that tree after 5 years just think how you would blow up. But if you give up yo will never know. One thing I really hate to see is any business fold, I never understood as a child why it bother me so but it did. If it was small business in the neighbor hood are a bigger business down town. It really bother me then and now to see that happen. I remember when I was growing up and the down town was down town and busy. Seem like just one day it went away and left the neighbor empty. I guess the business that could afford it left and went to the big mall some one had come up with.

But the little guys were left behind in a Ghost Town call down town Little Rock. Well all the real business left the little guys and they tried to sustain but there were slowly gong out of business, you know why every one went with the trend. They follow the big stores to the new malls with the bigger prices. That another thing about business believe it or not you have to be able to move with the trend, if not you want make it. Times changes and you have to change to in the business world believe it or not, I see to many business that can't are want make that transition and it cost them big time.

Some say they'll be all right, I not studding all of that, those business are foolish and want last. It seem hard but I seem to many that want make the transition are just want. Then they wonder why people are going else where, some say you know my people thy will support me, might be true the point of business is trying to reach a new customer everyday. This is how you stay ahead of the game if all you are getting are the same old customer then you are not growing. You just making enough money to buy some more of what they want and sell to them for a quarter more. Yo don't have a business at this point yo have a trading post.

In short in watering your dreams you have to be in position to keep on with the time also. Be willing to go to the next level, when you dream don't waste your rime with small dreams, dream big it your dream big as you want to sometime when you are watering that dream you may have to but a little yeast in in, ya! That's the ticket! But some yeast in it baby! & Blow up! Big!

CHAPTER XXV

YOU DESERVE IT!!

Jan. 24ᵗʰ 2014

Your dreams your wish, your vision you deserve them all. So go after them with all you got. Live to day like there's no tomorrow. Live to day just like your life depend on it, what because it does. Nothing in life happen by chance, no, no, that's barely the way it is. There are dreams and dreamers, the different in the person that dreams show no effort after he wake up. But the dreamers can dream with his eyes close and wide open. This is what it going to take to be successful. Dreaming with your eyes wide open.

Here's the deal the person that dream wake up and say wow! I had a crazy dream last night and it over. First of all they don't really remember what they dream about! My God the dreamers he/she wakes up wondering and questioning what's that's all about. Then the next thing you know there run and get a paper and pencils while it's fresh on there mind. See because just happen and they want to remember the whole thing. So they want to jot down all they came remember why because it was important to them. You know you deserve the best. There something inside that want let go, because it's in you. It's been there for awhile and you can't let go, it's been there every sense you were a kid. Some how you know this is what you allways wanted more, you wanted to be more you deserve to be more why because more has become more of you and you can't be satisfied with nothing less.

Just take time and think or write the things that you deserve in life, some of the other things that you are working for some one else to have. Like your Dream Home, Your Dream Vacation, Kids being able to have a great educations, even go to private school if you want, A Brand New car 2 if you like. Generations of wealth no longer have to wait and buy if you need it now. Kida see where I'm going with this. You deserve all the things you are working for some one else to have. Once you get a mind set that I'm as special as the person that I work for. Then you can start to move forward in your dreams.

It all start with you and what you really want out of life it's about you having that mind set that no one can destroy. When you learn how to see in the dark you are on your way. You have to see your dream come true on your worst day, when every thing is going sour and there's nothing looking good for you. I mean man it look like your dream is over basically. You just want to give up and become a normal Joe all over again. You feel like your dream is on its way down the drain. Hey I know this sound crazy but may be you have to get the plunger and make it come back up. This is call seeing in the dark when there seem to be no light at the end of the tunnel.

But on the real you have to see your way threw, because with life come disappointment. This is where you find out what you are made of, can you keep seeing what no one else see, believe what seem to be impossible to you are other. The Late Great Nelson Mandela said it only seem impossible until its done. Meaning things might seem impossible to you at time but when you weathering the storm, come threw the curves and waves that life throw at you. It's all possible! And now that you have made it happen you now know it's possible too. See people that go threw things are the ones that can tell you something about making it and being successful.

When you have some trying to tell you how to make it, but never held on to the struggle. It's hard to listen to a person like this, now take you for instance you were able to see in the dark. You went threw the struggle and you made it believe it are not you are going to make it. Your Greatness is what kept you wondering and kept you reading because you are searching for a better you. And really there something in you that want more, and you are loving it.

After pain and disapointment come success! Because there is success after pain. In other word there is good after bad, everybody may not have to go threw this way. But if you do it will all worth while. Any thing that worth having are doing is worth the pain. See what you have to figure out is this I once heard that 75% of you being success is showing up. Whether it's in school, work, business, are what every you want to do in life it's about showing up. How are you going to learn if you don't show up to be taught. This is how you become more great and knowledgeable, about what you are trying to do it's" showing up."

See when I got in the business of 5 Linx Home Base Business, in order for me to do good in this business I had to do what it took to get ahead. That was going to the meeting and making the conferece calls. See the same thing get the same thing, if you don't do it you want be successful at what you are doing. To many times people start off good but in just a little while, they loose there train of thought and they are back in a rut. Just like in this business everyone that get in is not going to make money. Not because they can't make money, it's because they want apply themselves to do what it take. They quickly for get there WHY! It sadden me when I see this happen. I rally like to see everyone do well but some are just meant to be average and that its' sad to say. But the truth is the light!

If you really feel that you 'DERSERVE" better then go for it. Instead all I hear from some people is complaints. Time is to short for why I can't make it, people spend to much time with excuses. If can see your dream no matter the what the struggle the better the chance you have to getting where you want to be. Remember you "DESERVE" THE BEST OF LIFE, JUST LIKE THE PEOPLE YOU WORK FOR!

CHAPTER XXVI

NO REGRETS!

Jan. 25th 2014

I hear a lot of people saying man, I wish I had done this are that! I wish I had followed my dreams, I wish I had finish school. Man I should have stayed with that guy/ girl. I wish, I wish, I wish! To me that's sound like a lot of regrets.

Sound like a lot of bad decisions making. You know it's life and it happen but some where down the road you should have learn how to make sound decisions. We shouldn't have to go threw life regretting we every lived, no, no, that shouldn't happen.

Some people do they go threw life, not being able to make wise decision and have a shoulder load of regrets. Some can, some can't handle them so what they do they take what they think is the easy road and exit there life with there own hands. What they have just done is creative a life in hell, that is really hell and there is no exit.

What we have to do is this is learn how to think about what we are doing in life. We should learn how to look at our self at an early stage and ask yours self is this the way I want my life to go. Just before you go over the edge tell the horse to woo! Woo! Horsey and stop right there in your track, don't move another inch. Now you stop and see what the direction you really need to go in. what do I need to do different? If you need some help get you some. If you don't know nobody that can help in the direction in which you are going. Then do like I learn to do and thousands of other are doing look it up on the internet. Seem to me that u-tubes seem to have a lot of info.

I found many guys that were able to help me in my adventure of life changing and you can too. But the best start I receive was the Bible. What I'm saying is don't go threw life regretting something that you actually had control over just didn't spend the time and make it happen. Don't regret not following your dream, because you let something get in the way. Yes life is full of adventure some good and some bad, even put you on hold sometime. Sooner are later it have to let you go, believe me I know it might takes years before the right thing come along.

But the fact it is, it will come along but you have to go and meet it. It want just fall in your hands. It's not going to happen it only going to happen if you are out there trying to make it to happen. I was doing a little talk show on the radio called "BUILDING DREAMER" about the Business we are in call 5 Linx Home Base Business, doing the fact it was a small program I had to hustle up my own sponsors. These were small business people so they had limited about of money. I was dirt cheap on the advertisement I just wanted them to help keep my show on every week.

Well you have to go threw the numbers to find one, and when you did they wouldn't pay like they should. Which had me kind of angry but you know that were helping me so wasn't much I could say. I was listening to THE HIP-HOP PREACHER E.T. ONE DAY ON YOU-TUBE" he was talking about it was your Dream" you have to make it happen no one else care about your dream, IT'S YOUR! BABY! IT'S YOUR DREAM YOU THOUGHT IT UP THEN YOU GROW IT UP!

So that's when I thought about something by now I should have known in the first place. Like my DAD! Use to say have your own son, you can't get mad about no one else money. You know what he was right then and he is right now. So here's what happen I made up in my mind I was going to so this thing, using my own money. If I find some one along the way that would help that's great. If I believe in myself and my show strongly like I want other to do then why not sponsors my self, to get it going and keep it going if I need too. This is one thing I want have to have regret over you know why? I believe in me and I believe with the help of the Lord we can make it happen. See whether you know it are not I'm never along, you never along! So that's what I'm doing and actually I find it less stressful. I don't have to worry about where the money coming from next week if it's coming out of my pocket.

I refused to let life get the best of me one more time, allow life to stop me one more time from letting something great happen in my life. It's just life being a director of an movie you have to step up and be in control of your life. See are so use to people tell us what to do it hard some times to make the next step with out being told. Time for a change and you have to make it no regrets baby. I rather fail at something than never tried in the first place. I don't to spend another day regretting what I didn't do or could have done. This is not the way I want my life to play out! See when you put in your mind your going to make it happen there no one on God green earth can stop you! You are unstoppable! At this point no regrets!

I remember back being young I wanted to be a Bass players, mom and dad bought me the bass guitar and I was happy as can be. Man I use to make noise with that things for a while never learn how to play it, even had an old man that was going to teach me free. Never took the time to learn how to play even though I wanted to play bad, but not bad enough, I guess I was just what I call a C.W.B. CAPTAIN WANNN BEE! To this day I still want to learn how to play this bass, I remember the bass player for Earth Wind & Fire this guy and guys like Booties Collin had to be the greatest. Man I love to hear and still do like to hear these guys play. Now I be in church and sometimes I just want run up and get the bass and start playing. But sad to say I don't know how.

I will learn how to play that bass and when one day the bass player is not in the choir, are if he have to play drums instead of the bass. I going to get up there and shock every one as my finger like up and down that bass guitar, as my finger pop those stringer of glory. That's going to be one happy day for me and surprise for others.

Yes! I have regrets for not learning that bass, I shouldn't have a life time of regrets for something I didn't do. The great things is this I still have a chance to go back and make it happen. So it up to me what am I going to do, it's up to you what are going to do with the rest of your life enjoy are regret! It's your life and your choice.

CHAPTER XXVII

EYE OF AN EAGLE, HEART OF A LION

When trying trying to be successful in life, when trying to reach a goal to make a mark and make something big happen. You have to have your mind set right, your target have to be on point. Have the eye of an eagle and the heart of a lion. An Eagle fly high and look low when he's going after a pry and sometimes he might not have but one chance to make it happen. See what he looking at might be looking at him, and knows it's in trouble when he come after him. So as the Eagle start to come after the pry the pry begin to run for shelter, the faster the Eagle flies the faster the prey run. So now the if the eagle want to eat he have to be on point, if the prey want to live he have to be on point.

So here we are in the case of only the strong survive, are in this case only the wiser! So we have to be like the eagle, you have to have your eye on your goal, you have to be sharp if you are plan on surviving, again you have to be like the Eagle you have to be hungry.

Now the Lion he have heart, he not scared to tackle nothing in the jungle. Might of fact he is known as the King of jungle. Just like the eagle if he going to eat he have to find his prey and most cases chase it down if he wants to eat. You know if he's not hungry prey will just pass him by. That the different of being hungry and not! If you are not hungry as you say you are, opportunity will just pass you by.

If you are hungry and want to eat, you will go out and make something happen you will find your self being a go getter. A lion will chase his prey until he can't run no more. You have to chase your dream the same way, if you give up it will never happen. That's when you start to settle for what ever, that come your way. You will never be happy about yourself again, maybe some people would be but you are not that type. See people like you and I we have some adventure in our life. We have to have a reason to wake up in the morning. We have to be working toward something positive. It's not our fault it's just something in us call greatness. It want let us be still when one thing don't work, we just find ourselves doing some thing else that want let us be still. This is how winners are made this is where skills come to work. Talent maybe skills no doubt, because what we believe and what we do cause for hard work. Talent is a gift and many are bless with it, but skills come from a blessing and hard work.

The harder we work at our craft the better we feel as it grow, you can proudly said that my baby! I might have mention before somewhere in the book, that only time success come before work is in the dictionary. In the Business of 5 Linx, people want to want to know is it hard? Yes! Anything that worth having cause for hard work! If you not willing to do it, I really don't want you on my team! The reason you are in the situation you are in now, is because some where down the line you wasn't willing to put in the hard work to better your life. The people you work did and now you are working for them. Now ask yourself what part of the money do you get out of that.

IT ONLY SEEM IMPOSSIBLE UNTIL IT'S DONE [Nelson Mandela]. You notice I like that quote, because it is so true. If you would just allow your mind the opportunity to stretch! Learn to allow more knowledge to come into your life. Get you a new set of friends that want to do something, better yet that already doing something. Since you are not doing anything show some interest in what they are doing. Hang around long enough they might just give you an insider on how & what they do this is giving your mind the opportunity to stretch and see, what they are doing is not so hard after all it's just about the mind set and just doing it.

I had to get out of the circle that I was in if I wanted better in life. In other words a change have to be made in your life a total make over. If you don't know successful people that all right you will once you become successful, trust me they will find you. Until then hey if you really want if you'll find a way to make it happen! I said you will find a way to make it happen. When I started doing similar on the 5 Linx Home Base Business, I didn't know what I was doing the truth being told. Someone had to lead and I knew if I was smart enough to read, and learn about the business from a few folks I could see my way threw. So I would do this every Tuesday nights for the team to try and keep them on track. But I to learn the business so I could answers the question thank God most I could but some where over my head. But I was honest I wouldn't fake it are just tell them something in other word.

I would promise them I would get the answers and I would, like I all ways told them if I didn't know the answer I would get it for them. Before I just tell you something I, would call the company and get the right answers for them as soon as possible. That along got me the respect from my team because I would do what I, say I'll do. They could have got the same answer I got, but they didn't want to make the call and wait on the line for customer service, but I would that help me to stand out on the team as a team leader because I, could be and still can be trusted.

Another thing I had to learn was to how to motivate people, that when I went to you-tube and looked for these speakers to see what these guy were doing and how. I went for help to learn how to help my team, and now you see how people become so successful because one thing lead to another. I went for help to help my team and I have gotton so much knowledge between the team and the movitaional speakers I found a reason to write a book. WOW LOOK AT GOD!

See this book was coming from a few note I was learning off the internet with these speaker. I would listen just about every day and jot down something that was important for me and the team. I would jot down notes also for my radio show. Just a few little pointer can go a long way if you know anything about what you are talking about any way. So I would do this and date it and save in the Lap Top!

Then one day the Lord put on my mind, if you going to right all of this stuff down why not just write a book? You might just be able to help some one, by what you learn from trying to help others, know what I say GOOD IDEAL LORD LETS DO THIS! WE HAVE BEEN WORKING TOGETHER EVERY SINCE.

You have to be hungry for what you want, you have to want it as bad as the Eagle & The Lion. THE EYE OF THE EAGLE THAT WANT TAKE HIS EYE OFF THEPRY[SUCCESS] THE HEART OF THE LION THAT WANT BE SCARED AWAY [FROM SUCCESS]

CHAPTER XXVIII

WRITE YOUR ON STORY!!

JAN. 26TH 2014

You know if the truth be told we can all write our own story, or some one else will! we can choose our destiny. We don't have to wait until we die for some one else to tell our story, when we can tell it our selves. "Lets play role a little bit" Just think if you follow your vision of going in business, and you were great at it. See because you believe in your self and went for it you become the multi-million air you wanted to be. You knew if you had a "B" plan that would just mess up your "A" plan. So you stuck with your "A" plan and one day you become so great that, people on talks show wanted to pay you to come talk them.

Sounding good so far! There you are on national tv been interview about your success. They ask you how you do It? And was it hard? You told them first of all I believe in me and I held on to my vision! Yes it was hard at time but I couldn't quit because I was not a quitter. Then you smiled and said I stayed with my "A" plan.

The question was then ask what was your "A"? you told them not to give up! Believe in your self! And it's all possible! Took some doing some learning, a lot of praying! In the end it was all worth while.

Then you may have been asked, if you had some advise to give to the next person coming up what would it be? I can see you smiling and saying if you have a DREAM! Stick to it never give up! Stay prayed up & focus on your dream! Keep in mind that it is Possible other have done it and you can too.

Here's the deal people we all have the opportunity to write our own story, it's our life but you know your life is as good as any one else. But what you do with your life is your business. You can wish upon an star all you want, and hope things work out for you are get lucky as some people say.

I don't believe that luck will have nothing to do with your success, it going to take a lot of praying, lots of hard work, having faith to work when you don't feel like it. Staying awake when you want to sleep remember it your vision so you had to work harder than any one.

Life is like being in a box when you work for some one else, you have no control and you can't stand it. Take myself for instance, I never got along to much with my boss. Some even call me a trouble maker. I really didn't understand why I couldn't get along with people being over me. So when you go and get a job they asked can you get along with others, and do you work good with the person in charge? So many times I have lied and said yaw! Just for them to find out I was lying. It would be all right for awhile. Then that something in me would flare up, and that was I didn't want to listen to no one tell me what to do.

There were years that I did, but Lord know I didn't want to, but I had a family. I was known as a hard to get along trouble maker. Not really it was just that something in me that wasn't going to let me live this life, with some one else writing me a small pay check for the hard work I was doing. That desire for me to be in charge of my life was there. I couldn't give up. It was like being lock up for something I didn't do and I wanted out so little my little I dug my way out. Meaning I couldn't never let go of my dream I was a dreamer and in real life they do come true. Now here I'm writing some of my story my self. Soon you will read the rest in my book THE WHOLE TRUTH"

All I'm saying is this you can have 'FREEDOM IN THIS LIFE" if you really want it. Some people are just scared of failure, some people are just scared of challenge,some people are believe it or not scared of making money. Far as I'm concern I'm BLESSED" I'm not scared of none of that. Even wit all the ways that we have of being successful if we work at it people want try but {but} there it is again. They still have the nerve to complain about there money, there jobs, and where they are living and what they don't have. To shut them up! Because I have no tears for them, I lay out the opportunity of a LIFE TIME before them called "5 Linx Home Base Business" I let them know how the business work, I let them know they can make the money they make it a year in a month if they work the business.

Then I let them know it's not an over night fix, but it's 'GENIUNE" & SO REAL. A way out of your "PRISON" sort of speak not asking you to quite your job do it part time. When your part time start paying more than you full time you know what to do.

First thing they want to know is it free! MY GOD! People I have to think to my self there nothing in life is free, everything cost some body but no. Then I tell them for less than $400.00 you can run your own Home Base Business and grow and never have to leave home again to go to work if that's what you choose.

But {but} there that word again, there minds have been locked, and controlled. They are taught now at this point to just complain all you want but do nothing. But don't you worry some one will write your story for you. It will go something like this. Work hard all his life, retired after 4o years of service @ Mr. Bozo place and then he come out of retirement just before he died and work for 8 years for Mr. Bozo son before he got down sick and died. You didn't write your story but some one else did! Where was the freedom? Where was the joy in your life, notice Mr. Bozo had a business a successful business why we know that, because you worked for him for 40 years, after retirement you work for Mr. Bozo son, Bozo Jr.

See this guy Mr. Bozo took care of his family and when he got tired of working, he gave the business to Bozo Jr. all you have to pass on was your bill it surely wasn't much money remember you went back to work. All broke tired but you had to go, because you were scared to make a change, you have to learn to put your singal light on and move to the next lane is the next lane it's call success and it's waiting on you to move over but it wait long.

CHAPTER XXIX

LIVE YOUR DREAM

Jan 27th 2014

Are you will live some one else this is an guartee. Because every business that have every been built start with a dream / ideal. If you are not working on yours then you are helping some else that is all ready in progress. There no excuses not to make your dream come true are put in to motion. Some say they don't have the money neither did many other billion airs before you. Some say don't have the knowledge well go get it, go back to school if you have to, go to the library, go to the internet. Or just go back to work and get what they give you. But when you do SHUT! UP! & quit complaining and go back to your quarter and work for some one else. I get so tired of people that are so scared to conquer there fear, but they will work out some one else fear so easy.

My God! Are you not tired yet! of not never having enough of nothing. Cash your pay check and is all ready waiting on the next one. Where do it stop & when do you wake up. There have to be a change in your life, but you are the only one that can change it.

You know people are really strange and jealous, I was in Sunday School and there was a discussion about Lazarus & The rich man and some how another it went to the left. The conversation got more on people and money, and what they should do with it. How the rich should give there money to the poor, and one lady had the nerve to say that the rich should give to the poor, and if they are doing it from the heart they shouldn't write it off on there taxes.

Well there are times when you have to be quit and just listen, so that's what I did. But Lord knows I wanted to tell her how foolish that was. First of all if they couldn't get no return on there money they wouldn't be giving out believe me. Are there would be a very limited amount they would be giving out that for sure. Now these people were mad about how some one give away there money. This was the craziest thing I ever heard, at that moment I could hear my daddy talk from the grave. Who use to tell me son have your own money and you want have to be mad about some one else.

My point here maybe rich people are just people in general can do more to help there brothers. But the bottom line is 'HAVE YOUR OWN" if you have your own then we wouldn't have to worry about what ever folks do with there money. In most cases we all have a chance to make it in life, but the different is some people don't want to go threw to make things happen. Some people don't want to take advantage of great opportunity. These people that was complaining about some one else money, was some of the same people I talk to about getting in the business of 5 Linx Home Base Business.

They didn't want to believe this was real, are they didn't have money, are they didn't have time. They had all kinds of excuses why they didn't want to go in business for there self are just stop by a meeting and see how it works. There no need to get mad because some one went out and work hard to make something out of there life. When all you want is a hand out and complain about how much some one give you. Get real and learn how to Live Your Dream. Stop depending on some one else to take care of you. I know we all have dreams of being more than what we are, but they some how are another got away from us. But you know what we still have the opportunity to Live Our Dream. Get out of your comfort and least try to better yourself.

I stead of finding out what we can't do, let try to find out what you can do. Here's the deal the different in a rich and a poor man. Let say there

2 average guys working every day both trying to save a little money. Now both of these guys are allways talking of making it big one. They have a little money in the bank to fall back on are waiting on a great opportunity to come along something to invest in. where here comes a great opportunity, a company on the ground floor. All you have to invest is $1000.00 now they both have it and it want hurt either of them. One gut thinking about it and talking to folks with no dream are money about this.

What's the first thing they tell this guy, man don't do it it's a scam. So after talking to broke folks with out a clue he decided not to invest and tried to get his partner to do the same not invest. But his partner just told him man this is a great ideal lets go for it, I'm being dreaming for a moment like this. He didn't talk to no one about this but his partner and didn't do much talking then because his mind was set and no one was going to talk him out of this. Well his buddy told him man so and so told me this guy is going to take your money and you want hear from him again.

Well he was right sort of speak he didn't hear from him again, but he have been receiving some real healthy check from this business. Now the other guy would like to get in but can't afford the stock now. See you have to take an opportunity of a life time in the life time of the opportunity. You never know when the next one will come along. Now the broke guy that was scared to follow his dream every time he buy from Wal-Mart he help is buddy check go higher and higher. Now he would like to buy but the price is so high now he can't afford it.

See how some people are just so simple it's crazy. You saved up to buy in something like this and when the chance can you ran from it. It still going on today people aare scared to Live There Dream, they act as though they owe the people they work for something because they gave them a job! Yes it was a blessing true enough all you owe in return is to do a good job and that's it. You don't owe them your life, you are just exchanging time for dollars. When you can no longer do it they will just find someone else and they will find some one else.

So why you still have breath in your body, 're you are still able to think and work then you need to Live Your Dream! Make it happen it's your dream & your vision. In most cases people want see what you see so why bother telling them what you are trying to do. Let me as a need to know Basic, and they don't need to know. The be like the guy we just read about that had to have every body thoughts. Instead of following along with his body, he listen to some one that didn't have a clue.

Don't miss out of a great opportunity by listening to people that don't have a clue! You can't Live Your Dream! If you talk to people that can only cause you to have nightmares.

CHAPTER XXX

PLANT A SEED {WATCH IT GROW}

Just close your eyes for a few moments, and think about something you really want in life! Think about what would make you happy, think about what is it that will make you so happy that you will let no one get in your way.

What is it that you will almost die for, this has to be it & because you want it so bad, your desire is so strong you have to have it... I want you to stay on that mountain now I want you to say it's [POSSIBLE] with out a shadow of an doubt I want you to say it with BOLDNESS IT'S [POSSIBLE] WHY BECAUSE IT IS!

God has allowed man to walk on the Moon, and he allowed Peter to walk on water. So I know he will let your Dream come true it's possible. See we have to see thing before it happen but in seeing you have to believe. A strong mind can believe and see it before it happen it's the faith that we have allow our will to do happen. I know some smart person may say well Peter walked on water, but (but) there it is again. he started to sink. My response to that will be & you will to if you loose faith along the journey.

If you put your mind to it you can make it happen, don't never say you can't do something before you try it. Go ahead get your feet wet you can do, it's all about planting a seed and watching it grow. When you decide to plant a seed stay with it water it nourish it and watch it grow. I think where people go wrong first of all is there patience. If they don't grow tree over night they give up, they may water the plant are they may not. Why because they loose interest real quick

You have to give your self some time, give your seed some time. It will happen but you have to have patience. Another thing I see happen since I been in this business of 5 Linx Home Base Business, is this people start in one business something else come along and they jump for that too, because it sound good and think they can make a lot of money. It's just like trying to serve to God & The devil you going to love one and hate the other guarteed. Why would you take on something else when you have not even sat a good foundation in this one.

If you love what you doing and that's what your are going to have to do, you're going to have to love it to make it happen. If you don't love what you do then you want do it long are you want be good at it. Just like a job you do every day, you really don't care about the job! But it pays you a little money are as some say it pays the bill so you stay there and settle. Then later on in life you are still there, because you say it pay the bill before you know there you are 35 + years and holding. But you are still talking about leaving this old job one day, yep! Just like you were 35 years ago!

One thing about life it waits on one don't care who you are where you come from you have the same 24 hours a day as everyone else. Some people just have a better way of using there time! What are you doing with yours. If you decide to start a business it is you that is in control it's your baby! You have to work harder, stay up longer, sometimes go with out eating if you have to sometimes you just forget.

I love listed to moviaters speakers, and I was listed to Tyler Perry on you tube. One thing he mention first of all was God, He said many of times people in the press would ask him how he's so successful and he would tell them it was God! With out him it would have never happen. Many times he have said this and many times it wasn't printed. But he said the truth of the matter is putting God first and these other things will come about Matthew 6:33 Love that scripture and try to live by it.

This is great and I love when some one of his statue have the BOLDNESS enough to admit it, there noting we can do by our selves. I threw that in for you FREE! Now the reason I hade went to the video in the first place and really got more than I was looking for. He was talking about watering your seed. I said seed not seeds here he was making a point that if you are going to plant a seed, start a business do one thing at a time and watch it grow. Find your passion and plant that seed and stick with it.

Don't start this business today and another one next week, and another one a week after that. People then really start to believe you don't know what you want to do. If worst you will be at the point you don't know what to do! After while you will find yourself doing noting just a C.W.B. that it and old wash up Captain Wanna Bee!

He was saying in short and I love this guy for this, pray and plant your seed start your business. Just like the farmer all he can do is plant his seed. He can do all he can do but the weather, sun, soil all depend on the Lord! So start your business but make sure this is what you want and then start to nourish it learning and spending time with your dream of being your own boss. Remember it's not an overnight thing, you have to steady pray about and work about to make it happen and it will.

This is the beginning of the dream that you like to live, go ahead and live it because you desire it. Your name is on it and since your name is on it, you have to satnd proud and do what God has bless you to do is be successful!

CHAPTER XXXI

I DARE YOU, TO SUCCEED!!

Remember when you were kids and you would be at recess, playing on the play ground. Remember you'll be on the monkey bars in the sand box, you would climb to the top and some one would dare you to jump. You would think about it but you wouldn't do it fear of hurting yourself. Then some one say to you he/she scared! Now all the little kids looking at you saying you a scary cat, scary cat. Now you'll say I'm not a scary cat I just not going to jump. Then you have that one, person said if you not a scary cat you'll will jump "I DARE YOU SCARY CAT" now we know the one doing all the talking wouldn't jump his self but he dare you! In front of every body.

The bell is about to ring and you have to go back to class and what every one is going to remember is you didn't jump cause you was a "SCARY CAT" SO WITH OUT FUTHER A DUE! You let go of the bars with out a second thought and there you were on the ground in the sand box! Suprisely you wasn't hurt and now you are the hero in the class because you took that plung! And no one else had did it yet now the fear is gone and every day you go out side now you go to the monkey bars to the top and jump! Wouldn't no one else do it for awhile so now yo are the King of the monkey bars.

Now I Dare You! To succeed n this Business of 5 Linx Home Base Business are any other business you go into. You have to really just challenge your self in life, with out the challenge life really wouldn't be no fun any way. Business can be great starting or working way can be great if you would learn to challnege your self more. Find more than one way of doing things each time learn to enjoy what you ar doing more.

I Dare You! To remember why you got in this business, I Dare You! To just think back on how your life was before you made that leap! You have to remember your why I Dare You! To check out the why you started something different, what every the reason was you had one. You still have one your just letting it fad away, please sir/mam don't let your life pass you by it will if you let it. Hit the brakes right now while you have a chance to stop the down fall. Back the car up and look in the rear view mirror, and see what you are missing you are missing the new live and opportunity that life have for you.

Want none of the things in life you wish for pray for,will never happen if you don't do something. Waiting on others will never happen! You have to do it are it want get done. It's your life and I Dare You! To take control of it.

I know sometime when you look at other, it seem like every thing they touch is goal. Just look like everything is going there way. They have that, something that every time some one say follow me they do where ever it may be. you just feel like some times God has looked over you and gave this guy part of your blessing (smile).

You know hat that's all good but we have to remember what God have for you is for you, what ever he gave that other person was for him. Have we stopped to think also what God gave him/her they used it. They found away to make it happen and they stepped out on faith no matter what and they made it happen.

You see how far you have read in this book, that tell me that God have given you that same something and you are going to have to do the same has they done step out on faith and make it happen. Stop quitting overtime something go wrong stop crying about everything that has happen. If you are going to cry after you have succeed in you adventure let the tears be tears of joy! Yo have it end you, just push it out. There a level of Greatness if you that you have not yet touch! But you have to either let it come out are it will bury itself in you! And when it do and time and years go by it's hard to get that fellow to move. What you have done is put your Blessing to rest, now it's just waiting on you to die, so you both can go to rest.

I want you to do something for your self, I Dare You! To move forward in your life pick up your dreams go back and work on them. If you don't think you worth it then do it for the spouse you say you love, the kids, the grandkids, just do it why because it in you and dying to live. I see so many people that are all hype up about doing the Business that we are in man they come to the meeting, yo can't shut them up there are so excited. The one day here they are not going to the meeting, not making the conference call. The excitement level have dropped to zero, then when you call them they have some sad story, why they can't make the meeting can't even sat at home and get on the conference call.

You know it's hard to ride a dead horse and if you try to get him up, by your self you will hurt your self. So when they miss a meeting or a conference call, and they text in stead of call I just text back "K" cause I know they are lying about why they didn't do what they where suppose to. Remember back when we were going to lie about something so we would call hoping we would get the voice mail. Because we didn't want to just flat out lie to that person and be question. Now we have the text it's easier to lie now we just T.A.L. Text A Lie.

I just made up in my mind just be nice say nothing just text "K" let you know I got your lie. Some complain that I'm hard, not really the case I just don't have time at my age to deal with stupid stuff, people that play games with there selves. I refuse to go down to that level its your money, do what you want but if you really need some help let me help you, if not leave me along see you when I see you! God Bless!

How in the Hell! Are you going to run your own Business any way if you want show up for your own meeting/ conference call. I don't have time to explain to you every week what we talk about. I might miss telling you something and the first thing that go wrong you will say that Jody said. I you miss regularly I'm not telling you nothing you are just wasting my times and yours. Only thing I will tell that was said was you need to come to your meeting.

I Dare You To come to your meeting, your conference call, talk to people, I Dare You to do what's right if you are going to make it. No need to waste my time or your if you are not going to do nothing but waste my time.

TAKE THE DARE! I DARE YOU TO! Get creative, about your self and your business look at you self where you are in life right now. Asked yourself are you happy even if you are, can I still do better? If the answer is yes! Take the Dare & do more better it's for you and your family and the ones that are coming. Some people can't see there selves in the future from where they stand now, they are in the dark and want turn on the flash light that's in there hands. That's not you, you want better, you desire better and in your desire you will have better.

Jump off the money bar of life and get busy, there a lot help out there for you, if you want it. If you are not doing nothing with your life really, there's but a hand full of people in there do nothing click know you and they can't help you out because they are afraid to walk up to the door turn the handle and leave that life.

So you might have to send out a sos! To get the help you need (smile) I really believe that's Success Is At your Finger Tips of those who want it! I DARE YOU TO REACH OUT AND GET IT "I DARE YOU TO SUCEED"

CHAPTER XXXII

YOU ARE THE PRODUCER

Jan 31ˢᵗ 2014

You are the producer of your business, in other words you are responsible for your life and business. The way it turn out is in your hands see when you produce something a program, a concert a movie if you are the producer how ever it turn out you are in the spot light. If it go good my God you get the glory, if it goes bad you get that too.

So that mean you are the one the cross all the it's and dot the It's it's all on you. The question is are you up for the game. People its time out for playing if you want to be successful and start working on your dream. Can't no one control your destiny but you, no one knows your dream your ideal but you. This is what make you the producer and only you can get credit, for what's about to take place in your life only you!

You have the power to change what ever is going on in your life you have the power. No one has the control but you, so you have to go forward with it. Get to know postive people is going to be important, here's the deal your business come before your friends. What are you saying Jody? I'm saying if your family are friend get in the way of your success move them out of your way. Get rid of them they are only going to hold you back. See you are the producer remember? People are depending on you more than anything you should be depending on you.

You have to get to the point that, I MUST, I WILL, MAKE IT! No matters what going on around me I'm in the mist of a mission trying to make it to the top. See you have to make it! Because your name is on it, your stamp mark your LOGO! This should be very important to you, because what you so today can enhance a better tomorrow. Never take your position lightly it's very important that you finish what you start,then people will know that they can count on you what ever the outcome will be. You will also so build yourself as a person that want quit. These are the type of people that others are looking for when they are trying to make something great happen. People can depend on you when they are doing project, they know if things are not looking good you want run away and tell them well that's you baby I'm gone.

See when you become that type of person, and when you start to build your dream and you look out for help you will look for people like your self. At this point you have trained yourself not to quit, give up, or give in, and that what you will be looking for in other people. In any business adventure any, you will all ways need a leader a strong leader.

See the team what I have found out quickly is only as strong as the leader. If the leader is weak no matter how strong they look the team is weak and will fall apart. The leader is like the producer and the team is depending on him/her if they don't put out the team want either, they are like a bunch of blind mice waiting to be lead. It's really not there fought it's the team leader fought, because they depended on that person to care them to the promise land instead he/she left them on quick sand.

What really get me when I, get involved in something that sound great and I have. Things are going good and then leader of the pack something go wrong in his life. All of the sudden he can't lead no more properly, this is not good especially if right now you are the guys with all the answers. It's just like being on the battle field you are in charge an all of the sudden you get scared and run back. What happen to the rest of the soldiers if they see you are scared? Now they see you running back they are going to follow your lead and run back with you. The same in business if you are the leader and can't handle pressure, are something go wrong in your life that you can't handle and then every one pay for your weakness.

It was at this point in the business field that I realize if you want something bad enough, you have to learn it for your self. Yes by all mean you need to learn for your self so when things go wrong your team leader fall dead sort of speak you can still go on. Remember the old saying one monkey can't stop no show. If you are going to be a producer then be a great one. There is greatness in every one some just want allow it to show. I have seen first hand what a weak producer / team leader will do, this is make the whole team fall. You have to be strong are just leave it along there are others that are in your life now depending on you. Is no longer just all about you, it's about others and if you can't lead/ produce leave it along.

I saw where these 2 guys were leading the team man we were on a row, people hyped some were making money all well. Man we were on our way to the top, people were joining up in the business that we were in, all was well baby. Then one of the guys lost his dad! Life happen I told you early in the book there are four things were going to happen in life, whether we like it are not. This was one of them you have to deal with it and move on. When my dad died love him to death, but here's the deal my job gave me 3 days off and back to work, sister died 3 days off and back to work. Brother died 3 days off and back to work. You don't quit work and let your team down take 3 days off and go back to the team.

The team can understand stand that like I said you have to be strong, When Obama was running for President I believe his Grandmother died, he took one day off and was back to work. No doubt he hurt like everyone else did, just think if had taken 5 days a week or more. One that would have shown him weak as, a want to be President. 2 that would have put way back on his campaign trail. 3 there were other people depending on him as well. We have to realize the one we love are not coming back, no matter how we miss them they are gone. One day we will be too, this is why we have to make the best of the time that the Lord allow us. When you and I leave this earth we are not coming back either. So our love one will take 3 days off and back to work no doubt. Then the other guy lost his dad and the same routine, now they wonder why the team is weak, I'll tell you why because we had depend on some week people that didn't understand 3 days off and back to work.

So what happen after this happen, people started to get like there leaders they got weak. If a person is all ready weak and you cause them to become weaker in most cases they never recovery and that what happen here no recovery. What I'm saying here is you are a producer / leader no matter what happen in your life if it don't kill you should be able to move forward. You are the captain, the team leader the PRODUCER!! Don't take no body life in your hands if you know you can't handle the first trouble that come your way. Life is to short for mess, if you can't give your best at all time leave it along.

CHAPTER XXXIII

PHENOMENON OR AVERAGE

Feb 2nd 2014

It's your choice that right I believe every one has a choose, on the way they live there life. If you choose the average life style that your choice, but that's what you get an average life style. That mean you work the average job, you stay in the average neighbor hood, your kids go to the average school. You first second if not all your car are used cars. You rent are lease your home, In most cases live at our below the proverty level. You take trips in stead of vacations your life is just normal, you get just what you ask for might of fact when you live your normal average life and struggle all the way through life, to top it all off when you retire and get ready for your golden years. What you do then is wish you had a better life and regrets all the years you did nothing but live average.

Because now you have to go and look for a job all over, see that what average people do. They don't get a chance to retire they work until they die, or they can't work no more. Don't take it harsh that's just what average people do, so you couldn't have expect anything different from what you got. Oh! You get a chance to say something over and over again, LIKE I WISH I HAD, BOY IF I COULD LIVE ALL OVER AGAIN, WISH I, COULD I, these are some of the sad things you will wish for in you later years. Keep in mind your best years are behind you now, you might have something left but I doubt it.

It best to get it are at least try to get it when you are young or at least when the opportunity presents itself. This is the different of the rich and poor persons, the poor person heard about a great opportunity and ran back and talk to some lifeless do nothing person about it. That person you talk to have no plans of changing his /her life they are settle in the mist of going no where fast. So what did you expect to hear from that person but [but] there is! Its' not going to work! Then they will go as far to tell you I tried that before and it didn't work for me. Ok! That might have been true. Here's the deal if it didn't work for that person there might have been a reason why. They didn't water there seed and took the time out to let it grow. Remember when you plant a seed it have to break threw the grown. You can't lay it on top of the soil and expect something to happen. Well it will it will blow away, and that's what happen with people that want what other have, but don't want to go through the trails and tribulations. Now the rich man heard of the same ideal you heard, but instead of running asking question and went and got answers and went to work. He planted a seed and was smart enough to know that it takes time to break threw the ground. He learn the business, he studied to see how can this work for him. He did what it took to be successful. People like to think that all rich are wealthy people were born with a silver spoon far from the truth. Now there kids and there kid and kids far off might be why. Because some one wasn't scared to conquer there fear, and went out on faith and made something great happen. It can happen to any one of us at anytime, put you have to learn to walk on water sort of speak.

You can't keep talking about and doing nothing about your situation, you know I learn to get away from people on jobs that just complain all the time. I tired of this job, I going to quit, this job sucks, it's not paying enough money. People like this along make you want to get out and try your own Home Base Business by itself. At least you want have to face all of those losers. I'm saying that because you are working a job everyone will have to work some where. We understand that the Bible says if a man don't work he can't eat. So that's not what I'm saying. I'm saying why complain about something all the time and never do anything about it. I have worked many of jobs, but you would never hear me talk about quitting.

You may here me complain about some of the people, as they complain about me too. But you never her me say I'm going to quit the job, although I was all was working on it. But until I was going to get paid doing something else I was going to be right there.

I heard at an early age if you want to keep getting what you are getting, easy just keep doing what you are doing I promise you nothing will change. I all ways heard that the same thing get the same thing, so don't expect different. See the average life is just what it is average, no respect at all. See what I have seem in the lazy life of average people, they get jealous of the one that live the "PHENONEN "LIFE STYLE' these are the people that wanted better and went for it.

This are the people that wanted a life style in stead of just a life. In there progress of success they became 'PHENONEN PEOPLE" NOT ONLY THAT THEY BECAME EXTRADOTARY! PEOPLE These people believe in there self chase there dreams with out giving up. See what I have seem in the past, present and future, the average people are all ways trying to get something from these people they wouldn't go and get there selves money.

We all have choices in life and opportunity in life to do better, but they REFUSE to take advantage of it. When great opportunity come there way, they all ways find something wrong with it.

Phenomena people go and get, average people sat and wait on things to happen. And they wait and wait and they are still waiting, while they phenomena people are going on with there life living large. Because you wouldn't go and get what was yours you will do with out and cause your family and generations behind you to suffer because you were afraid to use what God gave you talent.

I have to be honest with you, it really take a special person to step out of there safety zone. In the business that we are in we talk to a lot of people are some say something like I'm all right, I got a good job! My question is for how long. See you worked for some one else and at any time that place can close are down size, any case that can be the end of what you call a good job. People there are no guaretee when you are working for someone else. they tell you now that they are down size to make you feel better when they let you go. Laid off, fired, downsize all mean the same thing you don't have a job and there noting yo can do about it.

People with money know how to follow the trends of making money, that why when some of the people that are in the Business we are in 5 Linx Homebase Bussiness! Some are people that were all ready making 6 figures income, but they know they can do this and still make another 6 figured income to go along with that they are all ready doing see, we don't ask you to quit your job! We just ask you do it part time and when the part time start making more than your full time then if you want to you can leave,

Lady & gentlemen greatness is on you, don't be afraid of failure. You are only a failure if you don't try. When you try and fail that only mean you are getting closer to what you are after. I heard Less Brown say what you are looking for is looking for you. I say sooner are later you meet in the middle! NOW THE CHOICE IS YOURS!

BE PHENONEN OR BE AVERAGE!

CHAPTER XXXIV

NO REGRETS

It really is sad to see people that really had an opportunity to be great, and let it pass them by. Then one day they realize there mistake and it's to late. To often this happen and then people wish they would have listen. But that just the way people are, and some time we don't get a second chance. I remember coming up in high school guys playing basketball these young men were good but liking common sense. They scored high points on the team and they were winning games. They were really stoodout on the team every one love these guys, you know how it goes the high school hero's every one looked up to these guys.

Well one day the coach caught them smoking and that was a no, no, from the get. Then we had a hard coach that stuck by the rules no matter how good you were. If you were on this team you were going to play by his rules/ school rules, and one was no smoking. He meant that he didn't care if you were putting up 40 points a game. So he suspended these guys for a couple games. The school was mad about it looking at this guy as though he did something wrong but he was 100% right and we knew in our hearts.

These guys made it back to the team with the attitude they do what they want, started to smoke again got caught both of them and was kick off the team. These guys was heading toward senior year being stupid, I'm sure these guys could have played college no doubts who know could have made it to the pro's. once out of school the real life kicked in no scholarship no college, no fame. I know these guys regretted what they have done let something as little and simple as cigarette destroy there future. One did get a job with his dad the other turn out to be the neighbor hood crack head, which was very sad to see. I guess the morn of the story is don't live your life with regrets some time there is no second chance, some people have them many don't.

You know the old saying don't put off tomorrow what you can do today. You have to be real about your life, your future. Don't let little thing mess up a good life many people see good ideals and let them pass by and wish they had done something about it, but it's too late. I remember when Wal-Mart was coming up back in the day, I believe all you had to do was invest $1000.00. Well a lot of people got in, but there were some that found everything wrong with it, they were to scared to invest money to better themselves and there family.

They wouldn't invest and then try to stop other people from doing the same thing. I still hear people say to this day I wish, I had invested in Walnart when I had the chance. See now the stock is so high the can't afford it. When an opportunity of a life time come your way, there is no time to think about it's time act and act quickly. I feel so sorry for people that have to google every thing while they are google something trying to sound smart. The real people are getting in and ready to get going.

See the world is full of regrets people as they get older they get to the point where they feel like they haven't or didn't do enough in there life and they are right. The reason why they feel this way cause they know they didn't do what others did to take control of there life. They all ways wanted to wait till tomorrow, well tomorrow is here and where are you? The mess you were in 20, 25, 30 years ago nothing have changed.

Only thing change is you got older and brokers, and there seem to be no way out. So now all you have is regrets about things you wish had done. You regretted not going in that home base business we talked about. Now you old and vible cant hardly do anything for your self now you want to do better.

See if you do all you can do while yo can do it, in the end you will have no regrets. You wouldn't have to spend your latter years thinking about what you should have done. Regrets is a bad and sorryful thing you have to live with. If you will just go after your dream and make it happen. Just be a stand out type of guy/girl you can do it let the tiger in you come out. You know when a person really want something they go after it. Sometime you just have to make thing happen in your favor, others have done it and you can do it too. I'm not just writing are talking to you for the fun of it I like to one day hear from some one like your self. Telling me that my book was a help to you, my book is the reason you stepped out on that dream.

The reason you were able to conquer your fear, I would love to hear that I help bring out the Greatness in you. I heard some one say, and we all ways say in the Business of 5 Linx Home Base Business if you are not helping no one your not doing any one any good. This is why I want to help, I truly believe this and learn to live by this. You see where I mention 5 Linx Home Base Business a lot threw this book. Reason why I found out this one of the greatness network marketing business around if not the best.

There money to be made if you are will able and teachable, this business is making regular everyday Joe's like myself million airs. This is why I love this Business and want people like your self to become a part of this great Home Base Business. See because of this Business I will have no regrets, and because this is the business that allow me to take my life back. I want find myself on some dead end job I don't like. Instead I will be able to make money from home and you can so the same.

If you are really looking forward to making more money for you and your family. If you are looking for generation of wealth, working from home and making possible millions of dollars just go to my web-site. www.5linx.net/buildingdreams. Click on opportunity for more info watch the short video. Click on products to see what we sale in this business. Anything anyone buy off your sight, you get paid anytime they pay the bill you get paid as long as they pay the bills. You can sign up right on my sight and when you do I will call and talk to you and help get you on the way to success.

Trust me you can gain your life back why work a dead in job, that is not paying you the way you need to be payed to have a life style in stead of just a life. You owe this to your self don't pass up another great opportunity and live to regret it again. I'm looking for people that are looking, our team is call the Milllion Airs in motion team and we are on our way to the top. DO YOU WANNA GO! Again please don't spend your life regretting another great opportunity you pass up again. Get into the Business on my site and lets talk about your future 501.442.6899

REMEMBER NO! REGRETTS!

CHAPTER XXXV

FOCUS ON YOUR GIFT

Success is right at your finger tip! But if you look away at any moment are time you can loose it. See it's all about staying focus, on your career your success! Some time it may take longer than other. But that shouldn't matter how long it took the bottom line is you made it. Life have no guartee but one thing for sure if you don't go for your dream you will never make it.

You can't let other people pass become your future, just because Uncle Bob or Aunt Lucy tried it years ago and didn't make money at it, it don't mean you want. You know if you really dug into the old family secrets you might fing out they didn't put there all in it. You can only get out what you put in, no deposit no return.

Lots of people fail at what they are trying to do, because they want stay focus long enough and spend enough time on there dreams. We spends years and years watching other folks dreams come true, we even help them. But when it come to making something great happen in our own life we can't find the time. When you do this your are giving your power away! You are letting some one else control you.

When you give up on you what do you expect others to do? If you can't find yourself valuable no one else will. You have to have the power to stay focus on you your dream what's important to you. Don't understand why people will come out of slavery just to go back. You know when you work for some one else pennies on the dollars you have sent yourself back into slavery. Yes you have because now you went back to the slavery camp and said I want you to have power of attorney of my life. that what we do when we give another the power to tell us when to go to bed, when to get up how long to work, when to take a coffee break. We have given up what belong to us and that is freedom. Lets not kid are self we all know that ever one don't have the desire to do better to run a business, to have a dream home, a brand new cars, money in the bank,great credit scores, take vacations months at a time, generations of wealth is just not meat for everybody. But it is meant for those that desire it and say they want this type of life.

You know you will talk to some people and they will tell you I'm all rich in the Lord and I can understand that. That even tell you there father has a cattle on a thousand hills I believe that too. Then say something like my daddy is rich in heaven and I know that too. So explain to me why are you so broke if your daddy have all of this? Why can't you eat some steak some times why do all of your meals have to be hotdogs and nooles. So you are telling me your daddy have all of this and your broke, you must be the step child? I see.

To be one hundred with you, yes we serve a great God, and I believe that God will give us the desire if our heart if we will put him first Matthew 6:36. So quit being lazy and hiding behind God because you are to lazy to chase your dream. No one not no one will come to you and say here's your dream open it up and it's own baby! No, no that will not happen you have to stay focus on your dream plant that seed and nourish it and watch it grow.

Quit spending so much time on talking about what you can't do, and find out what you can do, find out what you are capable of, you never know what door be open for you if you quit complaining and walk out on faith.

Something what you are looking for will be all ready looking for you. But how will any one know if you don't put your self out there in the right place trying to make something happen. You never know some one might just see you working hard on your dream one day and say hey let me see if I can help this person out, let me see if can help them with what I know, if they see you believe in your self they just might have the money to help you. But you have to position and condition your self to make something happen.

Now be sure to be focus enough on your dream if no one never come up and give you a dime it's all right because you were going to do it any way right? Real dreamers, dream day and night. When things going good and when things are going bad they still have a dream to conquer. People like you and I we have gifts so we have to use them. If I never sale a book, I still did what I need to do to get it out there in the market place where it can be seen.

That mean a few things to me which is important, one I didn't let no one stop me. I did what I sat out to do write and publish a book. I stayed focus on my dream no matter how hard it got and sometime still I stayed focus, and completed my task. See now I can tell you to follow your dreams because I have and all ways will do just that stay focus and follow my dream. Because it don't stop with a book, it don't stop with me in my home base business.

See all of this is just another way on going for some more, I have to stay hungry! You have to stay hungry in the business world are you will just fade away. It's not that I'm greedy are unfaithful no that's not it. It just now that I know I can do this, let me see if I can do that! See you must all ways challenge your self to the next level there all way something to do in the name of Success!

It's the different of eating peanut butter and jelly sandwiches, or going out for a nice steak dinners or dinners of your choice sometimes. Only you can prevent poverty in your life, it all start with a dream/ ideal and staying focus. Other have done it and you can too.

CHAPTER XXXVI

WHEN IS ENOUGH, ENOUGH?

When are you going to be tired of living at are below the poverty line. When are you going to be feed up with the way you are living. There have to be a stopping point, but only you can be the one that stop the flow.

Time after time we see others around us do good, have good things. But you know why they have these things? It's because they believe in there selves and let noting are no one get in there way of success. You have to be the same way In your life of living here on this earth. You have to say to your self and only if you mean it enough is enough I'm going to change my situation. You don't have to be where you are unless you have just decided quit moving forward. Unless you just don't want anything else in life. There are people that will go to the limit to make great things happen, they want give up are quit on there dreams.

That's the only way your going to make things happen is by not giving up. You really have to be tired, you really have to get to the point that enough is enough. You know is kind of funny how people say they love you and care for, and then you asked for some money and the love seem to go away. There are some that might help you if they can, but still it's not there job! To take care of you and they want so don't expect it if you call to many time they want answers there phone.

See you can't get mad about no one else money, that there money they worked for it.

My daddy use to me have your own money, go out and make something happen save your money and beg no man for nothing. If you don't get it, it's no one fault but your own in most cases we all have the same opportunity to do better. I have one brother that have a little money, he went to school and made something out of his life and that was great. But one thing about this guy he was not letting his money go. Not to me any way see I was like the black sheep in the family.

I remember I asked this guy for some money one day, I was really in need and I knew this guy had the money. I for got all about what my daddy said, you can't get mad about some else money. When he wouldn't let me have the money I got mad, and in front of my kids he told me it's not my fault you don't have no money. At that point I said to myself ENOUGH WAS ENOUGH! I was going to make something great happen in my life and one thing for sure I would never asked this guy for a dime again and to GOD BE THE GLORY I HAVEN'T!!

He followed his dream and I have to follow minds, as I said before we are different people. Maybe school wasn't for me are it may not be for you, the great things about life is there are other ways to make money you just have to be tired of being tired. When you get to this point you will do better, why because you must do better. Success is waiting at your finger tips. Are you ready! For a fabulous life. Sometimes you have to Encourage yourself, give your self give your self "CPR" BREATH LIFE INTO YOUR DREAM AND make something happen. This is your chance your opportunity to make some good happen to you. You can have what other have, but you have to do what others do and that is follow your dreams.

You have to out set out on a journey of no return, no return of being broke, being with out, in poverty. There is a great light that is waiting on you, you have to chase your dreams no matter how far away they seem. The more you stay on that journey the closer you get to full filling it. You can do it why because you want more you desire more and you know that success awaits you.

Only the strong survive if you do nothing you'll get nothing. People that chase there dreams would sooner are later catch them. But if you don't chase your dream you will never know the out come. We are only on this earth for a little while, so tell me what will you Legacy be?

What will you leave behind when you leave, and you will leave. I mention once before we were not responsible for the way we can in this world, but we are responsible for the way that we leave. We all have a chance to make a different in our life time. Each day we live we live we are dying, will you be know as one that tried to make a different in your life time. One that wasn't afraid to make a change in your life. One that was thinking about your family when it was all over for you. Are will you be the one that just did nothing and nothing happen for you and your family. The one that was selfish and took all of your great ideal to the grave with you. Never be heard are thought of again one that barely had enough money to bury you.

The life we live are our own, there are times and times again when we can break away from the norm and do something great. So what if you don't have the money to do it, are you are not sure how to do it, remember if you want something bad enough, you will find away to do it. The Bible says we should leave are family an heritage, and in most cases we do they inhertiage our bills. That wasn't what the Bible was talking about. It really sad to see how so many people have just given up, and have settled for just what they get and that's not much. It sad to see how so many people are just living pay check to pay check. The money they make is barley enough sometime to pay a bill and buy grociers. There have to be a break point in there life you think, but they are so program to the norm. they can't see no further than what they see, and that's not much. I hear people say that they have a good job! They are sat but are they? As long as you work for someone else there will all ways be at risk! Of shutting, down, being layed off, cutbacks, down sizes, being demoited and what ever else that go along with working for some one else. If any of these things happen with your good job, then are you prepared to go forward, will you find another what you call a good job right away not likely. Just try to get you to wake up and smell the coffee because it is brewing have a cup!

People don't let life pass you by, don't settle for just a good life when you can have a great one. Take time and see what on the other side, before you judge others opportunities. Once you decide ENOUGH IS ENOUGH, you want and desire better you should go for it and make your dream come true. You already had a great part of making some one else dream come true, every day you hit that clock. So we know you can do it, so lets change lanes now and make your dreams come true!

Please don't settle for a little when yo can have a lot. You must decide to do better and do it. ONLY YOU CAN PREVENT PROVERTY IN YOUR LIFE!

CHAPTER XXVII

PLAN "A" ONLY!

Feb. 9th 2014

You know I use to hear a lot about a Plan A & B, I was like ok when one don't work try the other cool. Then I believe it was Will Smith and the Hip Hop preacher said get rid of the plan "B" it just away to fall away from what important plan A! see plan B really want get you were you want to be.

If you sat a goal don't work on anything else but that plan, and stick with it because it possible. Here's an example say your plan be is to become a big movie producers, you know it will take a lot of home work and hard work all together. But it will takes times and years sometime to make it. But your plan B, say if that don't work you get a job being a manger at a store or something. Nothing wrong with that but the 2 are a long was apart from being wealthy and just making it. Plan "B" just kill the real dream and before you know it again you just settled once again. So now I see there point and that's what I believe in just plan "A" throw away the plan "B" because plan "B" is not your dream it's just a substitute, and you will never be satisfied with it and you know it. Might of fact less for get about the B plan its' not important any way. What is important that you get an ideal and stick with it, don't let no one tell you, you can't make it happen. Its your dream any way tell the haters to stay away.

Might of fact like I told you earlier in the book, something some people don't need to know any way. They can't are they want help you so what is the use of telling them the direction you are trying to go in any way, don't give them the chance too cut you off at the bridge sort of speak.

Life is about finding yourself and what make you happy and stick with it. If you plan of being successful makes you happy then let no one stand in your way of happiness you deserve to be happy. See you are bless like that, you deserve to have the better things in life, might of fact you owe it to yourself to make it happen. When you discover you and the real you stand up and out, there will be nobody that can stop you now. When you have tasted the seed of success, all you are going to want is some more. You want just stop at one thing you accomplish your body your soul your spirit will hunger for more. Yo will soon realize all you need was a plan "A" and stick with it until something happen.

People that sat out to build walls or building, are smart enough to know it's one brick at a time, one brick at a time and one day the wall is there and has a great foundation to stand on. No matter how long it took are how many much man power it took now it up and can be up for hundreds of years. And that brick layers proud is one day years from when he/she finish they pass by and say with a smile I help build that building one brick at a time and it still standing.

See if yo just stick with your plan "A" and not worry about an "B" you will spend more time on "A" and sooner are later great things will start to happen. See when you only have one plan and that plan is to suceed, then if you are a go getter you want are can't quit because it's not in you. But if you had 2 plans you can easy walk away from the one that don't seem to work. I heard one speaker say break the rule not the law. See when you break the rule to go future to make sure you stay in the game is all right. Do what it take for you to make it to the top and stay there. People will tell you, you can't do it you a re wasting your time etc. etc. but don't let that bother you, what happen here is this, they are wasting there time telling you what can't happen. When you are spending your time wisely show them it can happen, that the different here.

There are 2 types of people in this world when it come to success, there are the one that are just waiting on the right opportunity to come. They wait and they wait and they wait and when the opportunity finally comes, they are not ready are no where to be found! They are the C.W.D., I talked about earlier in the book captain Wanna Bee's that all they are just pretending they are looking for better. So this what happen time after time when they let great opportunities pass them by then end up on an dead end job. Going to work every day talking about what they should have done, talking about how they are going to quit one day.

Then they are the ones that have greatness in them these are the proud ones and have the right to be. Because these are the ones that are creative, these are the one that finds ways to make great thing happen these are the one that love the big life and have a life style to show it. It's all about knowing what you want and making it happen, being the one that love the smell of success. Everything about you just say I got it! And if the Lords says the same I'm going to keep it. And all the others guys I spoke about all they have is a dead end job! That they hate and day they dread to go to work, every day they want to quit because they are miserable.

See the average guys and girls get the average jobs that get the average pay, they get possible 3-5% raise a year if they get that. It takes them possible 20 years to double there pay check if they every do. So when you do the same thing every day and don't have to use your mind this is how they pay you as though you are worthless even though, you are keeping there dream alive.

Now the dreamers can demand more they can and will make more, whether it's some one else jobs are one they creative. These are the guys that beat the systems, they more likely get 4 or 5 promotions a year. They will do one year what it took you 20 years to do if you ever do it. See these are the guys that stayed wit there plan "A" and made something happen. These are the guys/girls that wake up in the morning thinking different. How can I put my mind to work instead of my hands, how can I creative something different today. See because they know if they do the same thing over and over again they will get the same thing over and over again. They don't wait for things to happen they make them happen.

If you do the same thing over and over again you find your self in a rut! And it's hard to get out. I didn't say you can't get out I said it's hard to get out. See these are the people that are never satisfied with the last hurdle they jump over because they know there allways one more to jump and they are willing to do so. This is how they become successful this is how winners are made never satisfied with the last jump. They don't quit when the odds seem to be against them, they just don't do it, they know if there's a will there's away, and they find it. That the beauty of having one plan and one plan only, you have to make this work are yo just wasted your time and you are not that type of person, time is valuable and you know this.

So when it look like the odds are against you, when there no way out so it seem you have a way of making it happen. Why because there is no other plan that yo can fall back on this is all you got so you have to make it happen. See yo are the person that know 2 things and they are, [1] You can choose to survive [2] You can choose to succeed. Inside there are potential to suceed and you know it. The one that just survive are do just enough to get by don't get much out of life.

But the one that choose to suceed get what he/she want and more, why because he took the hard road. Life is like you take easy now, in the future it will be hard, are you can take hard now and easy later it's your chose. I can't choose for you.

I tell people at some of the similar we were doing in the 5 Linx HomeBase Business, that you have a side of your mind I believe haven't been use yet. They looked at me as though I'm crazy. I tell them that this side of your brain I called the green side haven't never been touch. God have preserver that for a moment like this, so you can think and think clear. This side of your mind haven't been touch yet, have been told bad things like, your never be nothing, your sorry, you can't do that, you are not smart enough are pretty enough, you are just down right ugly. Ok may be I'm going a little over board here. But the point I'm trying to make is this, you have a part of your mind that is free and the soil is rich and when you plant a seed it will grow. It's possible for you to grow, it's possible you can be all you want to be and more. Stay with your plan your one and only plan and watch and see that it work.

CHAPTER XXXVIII

WHO TOLD YOU THAT?

Who told you, you couldn't make it? Who told you that your dreams wasn't possible? Who told you that you was to old to seek your dream? Your not to old as long as you have breath in your body! But you need to get going, the only one you have to catch up with is you! People will tell you any thing but it don't have to be true, people will tell you, you can't make your dream come true, so what do you think! Ok that all that matters. You know it was once said and still stand to be true, those that say they can & those that say they can't in most cases are true.

I don't have to tell you that we all have a mind of our own, we all have choices to make in life. But when you start listening to people that have never tried anything that didn't have instructions, you are heading down the wrong road. There's no doubt people have ways of telling others what they can't do. This I find hard to understand because these are the people that never try anything that isn't easy. But they will tell you what you can't do, here's the deal life really don't come with instructions you have to be willing to try some thing and then write the instruction.

Be the one that stand out be the one that is not afraid to take the challenges. Be the one that go for it despite the odd that may be against, this is the whole fun of doing what ever they said you can't do. It's sort of like when I talked about earlier in the book. You know when I told you about the kids on the play ground and some one dare the kid to jump off the monkey bars and he did. You know what he then became the king of the monkey bars. You can be the stand out type of guy/ girl when you do what ever they said you couldn't do. You do what you do so good that ever one is talking about you, not only that now talk shows what you on the tv & radio to talk to them about what you did. Man I'll telling you that there nothing like it, when you do that thang that others said you couldn't do. It just the greatness in you that step out and made something happen no matter what no one thought are said. There is a joy in all of that! But the real deal is this you believe in you despite what the talk was. You went out and showed the world that you have heart and no matter what others think it's the God in you that can make things happen. You can be the king of the jungle sort of speak are the wimp of the house.

Real people that want a better life style don't let play people get in there way of success. Sometimes things don't all ways go the way we want, some times it may takes years are years to make it happen, but the important thang is really is that you made it happen. You know if I would had my way, I would have been at the top back when I was 19 years old. See that when it was all about me, but now I'm 55 years old and that desire of making it is still there and never left. But the different is now it not all about me, and there's a big different there. It's about my kids and grandkids and the ones far off after I'm gone.

You know just one day my picture might be on one of there walls and they will be telling there kids, ya! That old man started it all, he wouldn't give up quit are none of that so you need to be like your great pa-pa a go getter no one never believe he would make it no one but him. Now look at us all we have to do is keep the Legacy going, because the path has been laid out, the direction is all ready put in place. All we have to do now is follow the instruction that the old man left. Here what I said here! All they have to do is follow the instruction that I left, see because I wrote the book I started the 5 Linx Home Base Business and the instruction are, is to just follow the direction that I will one day leave.

And in that package of instruction it was say "WARNING DON'T LET NO ONE TELL YOU, YOU CAN'T DO SOMETHING" only you know what you maybe capable of only you! See that the different in a man with a plan, than a man that just a C.W.B. CAPTAIN WANNA BEE, THERE ARE TO MANY OUT THERE. See the easy way out of doing something is just doing nothing. One day when you finally wake up from the night mare of doing nothing you will realize that you have nothing! Because why you were scared to try and do anything, and life just passed you by.

I don't know about you but me it had got to real embarrassing to have to borrow money all threw life. You know I would all ways remember what my daddy said have your own. You know when you keep asking to borrow money from people then they want to know what are doing what yours. It make you mad because half the time I couldn't figure it out my self, on the real to be one hundred didn't know.

When I was smoking and drinking and running girls, at least I had a better ideal where it went. But look like when I got save for some reason that part only got a little better. I guess my problem was that I wanted to be somebody so bad that the little money I made just wasn't cutting it. But still I refused to let the position keep me down, the disbelief in me my other people keep me away from my success no matter how old I had gotton to be there was still that something waiting on me and I was determined to get it no matter how long it took. I was going to make it, I told my mom not long ago I was going to be on Ophry Whinphrey Show she laugh and said ya! Right!

You know I didn't just say that I believe that, I know she had a book club and I was going to try and get this very book in her face and then the other one behind it that was already wrote see what happen here I have a plan (smile).

Not just hoping something happen, but try and make something happen. See I wasn't going to let no one tell me I can't write this book, nor I can't get this book to Opry Whinphry if it don't happen it want because I didn't try. But where there a will there is a way.

CHAPTER XXXIX

THE VOICES IN YOU!

Every had a thought in your mind that was kind of puzzling to you and then that little voice come in and speak. I called it my first thought are first mind, are just plainly put the Lord talking to you. The funny thing about this is, in most cases it's only going to happen once. You don't get a second chance, in most cases it a split decision and it have to happen right now and the choice is right away. What happen in most cases we don't listen and make a bad decision and it over. Then the first thing that come out of your mouth is, I should have listen to my first mind. You know what you are right you should have listen because the first thought is normally the right one mostly in my case any way.

I have found in many cases not listen and made bad choices, and the first thing that come to my mind is man I should have listen to my mind. You know as you read this I know there have been many times you have made the same mistakes. But I was all way taught when you know better you do better. So here's the deal the little voice have been talking to you for a long time now, you are working a dead end job and you know you can do better. You know you been having a plan for a long time to start your own business, because it's just in you. And you are tired of being tired of not having enough at the end of the month, you are tired of the job that you have and you are hearing rumors about lay off, cut backs shut downs this is enough all my itself to give a nerves break down.

To top it all off you go to work and you have to deal with someone, that you trained for the job you should have. There a sign right there that you should have been gone a lone time ago. Once you realize the truth the truth will set you free, and the freeness of it all will give you freedom, it right at your finger tips. But you are afraid to step out on faith, the little voice inside you is telling you to go ahead and try something new. You don't have to tell the world just work on it and let it happen, only those that need to know will. But you have to follow your mind if you want some thing good to happen in your life.

Will you take your great ideal to the grave, because you are the only one that can do it this way. The way the Lord plan on you to do it yes it can be done if you choose not to do it. But here's the deal it want be done the way the Lord wanted you to do it because that way was for you and you only but keep in mind it will be done with are with out you.

When you hear that voice inside of you telling you to go ahead, you need to listen and go with your first mind. Some will tell you, you are crazy man stay where you at. They will even tell you, you can't do it! Here's the deal on that just because they failed at wht they were trying to do, don't mean you will. So what if you do fail a few time so have many people and they mage to get back up and try again. Each time you fail you get back up, why because you are now getting that much closer. As strange as it may sound, you are getting closer each time because you are now learning what not to do! What works and what don't work it call failing to suceed in most cases. Many people have failed and they get back up and get it right and one day they have perfected what they were trying to do.

So that's what you have to do keep on keeping on listen to the voice in your head that telling you, you can do it. You have greatness is you! Let the real you stand up and shine, why! Because you are not a quitters, that not you. Just listen what the voice is telling you. If you quit you didn't just quit on you, you quit on the family, and the generations behind you that are coming up that needed some like you to make something great happen. See it's the voice in you that telling yo that your family depend on you and you have to make, no matter what you have to make it.

Others have did it and you can too, yes there are hills and valleys but at the end there's also success waiting on you. There's a reason why God give great people like yourself dreams. The reason is he know that you can handle them, he know that he can trust you with something that is going to be a blessing for you and your family. He give you these dreams because he expects you to follow threw with these dreams. He know you can do it, if you will just trust him. I believe that the Lord will never put more you than you can handle. So there for when he gives you what you aske for and that is a blessing.

See we have the attendances of asking the Lord to show us a better way, and when he do instead of acting on it we start asking questions. There where the problem begin and never stop in most cases, we never get any thing done because of the questions. Instead of listening to the voice in us, we go and hear the voices of other people that had nothing to do with your dream or nothing else you asked the Lord for. I try not to get to bible on you, but realize this is the beginning of everything. Remember Noah! God told him to build an ark, he told him how tall and how long and the way to build it. He then told him in the meantime to preach that it was going to rain.

He didn't go and ask no one was it going to rain for forty days and forty night. The voice in him had already told him that it was and he believe that and that only. When he told him how to build and what to build with he didn't ask was he sure are not, if that was what he wanted he just did it. I believe that where the commerical come from Just Do IT! And that's what he did. And while he was building this ark, he was preaching to the people that it was going to rain.

No one believe him either but he kept on building the ark. And he kept on preaching because that what the Lord told him to do, so that what he did. This ark had to be least I believe at least 10 football field long and it had to be able to weather the storm for forty days and nights. It also had to be able to float over the highest mountain so it had to be right. Keep in mind that only did it have to be able to hold people but the animals from small to large, 2 of each male and female.

After all of that he didn't tell him to build it over night, it took him over 100 plus years to build it so no one believe. The same in your business it may take you a long time to build it so people stop believing you, and some time people stop believing in there selves because it don't come over night, or as quickly as they like for it to come so they give up and settle for what ever, less than what they are worth in most cases. When they give up it's not just them it's there family they give up on also. How because in most cases you are sating a bad example for yo and your kids you are telling them it's ok to give up on your dream, yo did and believe me they will to. So now yo just killed another generation all because of what you just done.

Walked away from what you believe and prayed for, all because you quit believing the voices that were in your head that was telling you, you could do it, that was telling you to let your greatness shine, that was telling you, you were not a quitters that was doing everything possible to make you go forward but you quit. So all you do now is talk about if you would, could, have listen to the voices in your head when you had a chance to make something great happen. When you had the money to invest in your self and you didn't.

If you don't invest in your self then who going to believe in you? When I started to do my radio show Building Dreams it was hard to get people to invest in me, as sponsors are advertisers. They didn't know me are where I was going with this, I was kind a pist at first. Started to saying dumb stuff like if I was white I bet these people would invest in be with no problem. I was about to have a pitty party with me, then I was listening to the hip-hop preacher one day ET, Eric Thomas. Love to listen to this guy to and he was saying it's your dream you invest in it.

You believe in you and you believe it will work then spend your own money and make it happen. So that's what I started to do was spend my own money sacrifice and make something happen. When I heard this I thought yo know this guy was right it was less stress for me to spend my own little money now to make big money later. Than it was for me to spend the week trying to knock down door just to hear people lie to me over and over again every week.

Hey I want to do it, it sound good but can you come back, next week, next month, hey buddy how about next year! Cool, ya! Cool. So it was getting to be a little crazy for awhile and when the Lord let me hear this I was like ya! Cool so I have to go with out a few things for a little while and may be when I get it going and get this book to start selling people will see that I'm serious and they will come to me. One thing about people in business they like to be a part of something great. Then they can say oh! Ya! You hear that show on the radio with Jody Luv! Building Dreams Ya! We a part of that too.

It's all good if you think I want let them in you are wrong, you know it's still good to spend some one else money. When you try to make money when you can, it's just good business this ideal was here long before I got here. I just trying to go with the flow.

CHAPTER XL

KNOCK! KNOCK!!

Who's there? Opportunity! Knock! Knock! Who's there? Opportunity!

Knock! Knock! Who's There? Who's There? And you finally look out of the door and there's no one there.

Again you let a great opportunity pass you by, why! Because again you were afraid to answer your calling. Opportunity is calling on people daily, but they are afraid to answer. I can't figure it out, they have the knowledge they pray and they wished for it! Some even went as far as to pray and fast for it. Then one day it come to there door the Lord have answered there prayer and they want answer. Or it's some time they tell opportunity to wait and let me call some one. And when they do it's all over, you don't need some one else advice.

You remember you prayed, fasted, wish & hope and now you need some advice from some one that know nothing. I can just see opportunity waiting outside the door with his head down, saying I still be in the cold when he/she get back. So I might as well leave now. So that what happen opportunity never get a chance to work in your life why! Because you want let it. You need the approval of others for some reason are another help me figure it out. I don't and will never understand why some one else decision is so important about what you do with your life.

Its your life they have there needs and you have yours, and if you need something from them and they need the same thing, tell me who needs are going to get filled.

Believe me it want be yours if they have to use there last, it take me back to dad again. he all ways says have your own. This way you want need much in life that you can't get your self. And this will also put you in the position to help others.

I tell people all the time in similars, THAT OPPORUNITY WILL NEVER STOP KNOCKING! BUT IT WILL PASS YOU BY! AND THAT YOU LET PASS BY, SOME ONE ELSE WILL SEE COMING AND TAKE ADVANTAGE OF IT!

So why let some one else get what you could have had, you shouldn't run from opportunity, you should run to it. If you are scared of failure you are going to have to learn to fail to succeed, many people have done it and yo can you too. Not many successful people didn't fail first, you just see the glamour part of success. You didn't and don't see the part where they almost gave up but decided they would never know the truth of the story if they did.

They are times when yo have to push up to get up! You can't lay there waiting on some one to help you up. People are busy and trying to take care of there own business not yours. In most cases you are not important to the other person I don't care how much they tell you they love you. When it come to departed from that all mighty dollar bill, you will see the love go the other way, quick, fast and in a hurry.

I use to hear a guy in church all the time talk about helping our brother when they are in need. Just ask my brother and I will be there fore you. Well there was a day I asked I need $10.00 to get some gas so I asked I thought it would be ok, since he open the door. We were talking and in the mist of the conversation I asked for the 10. And the brother stopped talking to me, and went to talking to someone else. I was like what the hey! This brother just turned his back on me, and started to talk to some one else as though I wasn't there. On the real I wouldn't have never asked if he hadn't open the door earlier but he did and he close it to far as I was concern. See he never thought about it again, but you see its still on my mind because I'm writing about it.

This is the very reason my dad say have your own and you want have these types of moment. You want be wanting to get mad about no one else money that they worked for. See this is why when a great opportunity come your way don't let it knock but once get in on it while its there and it's hot. A great opportunity can only last for a life time if you, make it last for a life time, meaning if you grab holt to it and make it happen for you and your family.

The problem I'm seeing in people going into business is this, there have to be excitement, there have to be excitement! I see people that are very excited when they first start man they are going to make this business blow up sort of speak. The momentous is high and blood is pumping fast and ready to make a million. But by the second are third month they seem to lose there momentum, they seem to lose that fire they had when they first started. Some can last a little longer than that, some might last a couple of years are so and then you see people just give up.

If you are going to be a winner if you are going to be great, if you are going to run your business you must have patient. You have to be willing to stay there and make it happen no matter how long it may take. 5, 10, 15 years what ever it take you should be willing to make it happen, it's your business your dream. You think guys that play football, or sports in general became millions airs over night no! NO! that's not the way it happen. Some these guys and girls started from pee wee sports before grade school so we are talking about 18 + years of believing in there selves. Having a dream that they held on to, they wanted something out of life and they worked hard for it. If they didn't go pro! All of them couldn't they still learn a value lesson and that is team work. And not only that they learn how to build something and have patient doing it. This is something that we all have to learn. To start and to finish what we start no matter the mountain are the valleys it don't matter, it's your dream do it.

You will now have something that you can pass on to your kids and there kids, because you have the experience of having patient. Quit living to die, and learn to die to live. There's something out there you want to do then make it happen, it's your dream your ideal no one can make it happen like you can, you are the author of that dream then you have the right to be the finisher. You and only you should get the right of seeing how that dream that ideal come out. You are powerful and,you know it why I believe in you is that you have made it this far in this book, why because there is something that you really want to do. I believe you need to get up and go to the nearest mirror and tell your self I'm a bad boy/girl. That right! I'M BAD! I'M SO BAD THAT I CAN DO ALL THING, IN CHRIST THAT STRENTHEN ME! SO I KNOW NOW THAT IT'S ALL POSSIBLE! I CAN DO IT! & I WILL. KNOCK! KNOCK! WHO'S THERE? OPPORTUNITY! COME ON IN AND LETS GET BUSY!

CHAPTER XLI

QUIT LIVING TO DIE

Learn how to die to live, we all know that every day we live we are dying. This is true from the first moment we breath our first breath any day of the week could be our last. So why not celebrate every day we live trying to make something great happen in our life. We should spend every day of our life as though it is the last because it can be. So why not enjoy your life, why not try to have some of the things that we want out of life.

Why not try and reach some goals that you have sat for your self, if not for you maybe for the ones that you love. Why go threw your hold life with out, with out money, with out a piece of mind, with out living the life style that you should have. People are living to die, no hope, no plan, no dream just living waiting one day to die. Actually if you don't have a dream you are all ready dead just waiting to be pronounced dead legally. When are you going to wake up and smell the roses, while you have a chance to smell them.

Have life really got that bad that you are not able to dream, man you can't be serious! People have learn to settle in there un happy life style, just like a hog settle in hi s slop. We have to learn how to live again, think back to when you were young and you had all of these great ideals, they were yours and they still are so look back and get you some of them and start working on them over again.

Why are you killing yourself doing something that you know you don't like doing? Follow your passions its not to late to get back to what you love, that's your dream. You know all threw this book I talk about not letting no one keep you from your dream. Don't spend your life dying when you can be living, when you can be have the time of you life. You can live like your boss, or whom ever dream you been taking care of all of these years.

People go to work every day just to complain about what they are doing. They hate the job and some even hate the people so every day they work, they are going to quit. Maybe you are one of those people that are going quit and do what. You have no plan why! Because you haven't took time to make one. You have to have a plan! Not a plan A & B! no! NO! just a plan "A" and make it happen. There is greatness in you there is success in you just waiting to come up & out. See you are already in plan "B" that's, the one where you go to work and work like a slave.

So we now know that plan "B" is not going to work, this is why yo should work on your plan "A" no matter how long it takes. You have to have some believeth in your self not the people around you but in you, this is what going to give you the strength to make something happen, see when people are tired, really tired of there surrounding are there situation that when they really put forth the effort to do something different in there life. That when they really start to think about what they are doing and want something different.

I was all ways told that an insane person do the same thing everyday, and expect something different, the same thing get the same thing DUH! If you go to work for the same employee, everyday, work the same hour, do the same thing and then expect your check to be any different than it was last week you are in sane! Yes! You are you are the craziest person on your job. There have to be some level in your life where you want to see a change on your check every once in awhile are something.

But the only thing that might change on your check is just maybe, just maybe you might, you just might get a Christmas Bonus are something, just maybe! In most cases most job have even cut that out. You know why they figured you are not worth it, how they know because you worked for them for years and they barely pay you anything but you just keep on working, & working yourself to death for them with no good results at the end nothing to look forward to but retirement and the rocking chair and if you live to long after retirement, you have to go back to work. Why because social security don't pay enough for you to stay home the rest of your dying life.

There are people out there that are scared of changes, there are scared for two reason. Some are scared of failure, some think if they fail they want be able to handle it, other think if they suceed they want be able to handle it.

Lets discus the failure part first and then the other, people are so afraid of what people might say if they don't make it the first time around. Well think about it the first time around is just what it is the first time around, many people have failed in many things the first time around. Some maybe have tried something more than an hundred time before they figured it out so what. The main thing is they stayed with it they didn't give up. This is how you become successful not by trying something one time and it don't work, and then some one make a big joke out of it and you give up! Shame on you not them, because they are doing what they are known to do, nothing but act silly.

You on the other hand you have a mission to work on, and the only way it really want work is that you want work on it. See the mission is not impossible unless you make it impossible. You have the control of your destiny and the only way something don't happen if you don't work your plan and stay with your dream. Dreamer don't let there dreams die, that when you become a failure not because something didn't work the first are second time. I was heard the only way you can get rid of a hater is to hang on two your dream and make it happen for you. Then you can show not only your hater but the world massive success. That what I'm talking about see after all of these years of me talking about making it big no one really ever thought I would do it.

But see there was something implanted in me a long time ago, that made me believe that I could be successful, that I could make my dream come true. Was it easy? No but it was possible, have I failed at times sure I have

I'm 58 years old now I thought about rich and famous when I was about sixteen years old see how long that been for me ha! Ha! One thing about money if you make some one surely will spend it that for sure. I pray to the good Lord above that I be able to enjoy some of it myself.

See the other great thing about holding on to your dream is this, for example I have many of kids and some of them have kids. So just maybe if the kids don't think like I do the grandkids will. Maybe a few of them will be dreamers like there pa-pa and say you know pa-pa payed the way for us to have a good life and all we have to do is keep what pa-pa started going that the great thing about starting something in your life time.

That the kids, kids can live and work off of if you see where I'm going with this. Don't be afraid to fail because behind failure is success not only for you but for kids, kids there ought to be a good feeling knowing when you leave this earth, you have put something in place for your family to live off of. To many times we leave broke and cause I'll family to be in more debts trying to take care the mess you left behind.

So many times our family member are not only crying for your departure, but because of the mess you left them in when you departed.

Now the other case is this it's not failure they are afraid of it's success. What you mean Jody? Let me give you a little story that I heard about a man a God fearing man at that. It's sad but it's true and the guy was just honest so I will give him that. Here's a guy that worked on a job making a little money, believed in paying his tithes & offering to the church, every Sunday like clock work. He did it because he was a believers and he did it out of his heart, so when he started to pray for another position that was coming open on the job, I understand that was paying over $100.000.00 a year the Lord bless him with it because he knew this guy could be trusted to do what was right as he all ways done. So he got the job and he was paying his ties and offering to the church as all ways. The problem was for some reason he didn't want to pay that much for some reason, he didn't want to cheat God, he just didn't want to pay that much. But if he knew if he kept that position that what he was suppose to do still pay his ties and offering.

No one was making him do that! But keep in mind this guy was a believer, but he just didn't believe for some reason he should pay that much. So to stay faithful to his believeth he decided to ask for his old job back step down from that new job. So he could once feel comfortable again paying his tithes & offering.

I guess the saying is true the more the Lord bless you with you should be able to bless others. See some people are being funny about being successful that why some don't worry and just settle for what they get and live with it that's there choice I guess. Some even feel guilty about being successful, why should you feel guilty about something you worked hard for unless you stole your success there is no reason to feel bad about something you worked for not at all. If anything you should be thanking God for Blessing you to get ahead in life and pray that you do what right so you can stay there.

Choose to live, not to die! Live your life as though there is no tomorrow. Greatness is in you and you and only you can let the greatness in you live.

CHAPTER XLII

STRETCHING YOUR MIND

Here's the deal the real deal the young folks have a great opportunity to make something great happen. Some times we have to leave them along if we can't help them. I mean in the business sense, I believe if you can't help them, then leave them along if you aren't going to send them some where to get some help. If you don't know then say you don't know and try to send them to some one that do! Nothing wrong with that, now the older folks like myself that have worked for someone else for years doing the same thing over and over again and getting the same results.

Now to some of the old school guys my age might be hard for you to change. The reason why it wasn't hard for me because I never thought working for some one else was for me any way.

But there are others to be honest young and old can't see nothing else but to work for some one else. Why because it's easy in most cases you don't have to think, it's all thought out for you all you have to do is do! What they say, when they say and how they say. All of the thought process is done and they don't want you to think are use your mind, because if you start to think you might think about leaving and starting your own business. That why they don't want a thinker they prefer to having doers.

So that what happen for years after years the plan is layed out for you to do. So one day when a great opportunity come your way you will be afraid of it, because now it cause for you to think and use your mind, something you really haven't done for years. So when a great opportunity come by

151

all some one have to say is man you are crazy to leave this good paying job for that. And before you know it you'll say you'll right and let a great opportunity pass you by. Then one day that great paying job you thought you had, that you wouldn't leave left you with out a second thought about how you would take care of your family.

All I'm trying to say again is there is no longer a thing call job security, no matter who you are, are whom you work for it's over. This is why you have to still be able to stretch your mind, be able to let your mind asbsorb new ideal. Don't be so quick to say it want work if you don't at least check it out, what didn't work for the last guy might be the thing that make you a million air. You can't go by what people say learn to check in on an opportunity for yourself. Keep in mind the person that said it wouldn't work must have at least tried it for his/her self to be able to tell you what they, think about it.

Then asked your self then why didn't it work for that person? What type of person is that person from the beginning. Is he or she the type of person that will give it there all? Are just try for a moment and quit? See I all ways have been the type of person that try things for my self I had to know first hand, if it would work are not. I pray that you are the same way when it come to your future. Here's the deal we have been told what to do and how to do so long some have just settle for that type of life. We are scared to do what the person have done, that you are working for. That's believe in there self and took a chance on life, and ideal, and invention, or creating something that can change there life and whole history.

But if you have not got to that point yet and still are looking for better, you still have the ability to want to dream and still have them. Then you know you should allow your mind to stretch, it have to be able to stretch and gather new ideal. Look for new ideal not be afraid to run with them, get want nothing people out of your life, pick up your dream once again and run as fast as you can with it. Get away from people that just want to work on the line, and talk about nothing all day. This is not you how I know this, and not know you? Because you have got this far along in this book, because you feel the need to change, and change is good. Your hungry and your tired of eating the same food, that just feel you up.

You want something that taste good and make you feel good, at the same time. That's is what you want out of life because you are different, than the one that have just settled. You don't want a little money to put in the bank, you want to fill the bank up! You want to fill your account up, you don't want have to do like I did for years check the account before I withdrawn. I wanna known what ever I want to take out in in there. What ever I take out there's still plenty enough left to take care all my needs. I wanna be like I have 99 problems but money is not one of them! And then and only then you know you are living, just saying. To let know one make you think it is wrong to have or make money. People who think like that are mostly broke people any way and want you to stay broke with them, so they can have friends. Remember misery love company.

Let your mind have a fresh look on life once again, this time tell your self that we can do it! Not I think we can do it but we can do it! And this time you don't stop! do not let up for no one are for no reason. Let the world know that you are coming threw like a train with no breaks and you all ready coasting at 75mph. So get out of the way because if I hit you, I have no ideal where you might land. See this is the attitude that successful people have when they are on a mission to make something happen. You are great and great people don't let failure of no sort get in there way. No stumbling blocks, no mountains, no low valleys they all are not move able.

See if you allow your mind to stretch and believe you will find out that there is a green side to the mind. I like to think of it as a part of your mind that the Lord preserve for this moment for when he thought you were ready to accept, the new you that believe that all dreams are possible if you put him first and then these things will be added. I believe this side of the mind was off limits to all of the other things that you heard that was true and un true. To all of the disappointment that you had, the sad days and moments that you had, the you can't do it that you heard and believe. Your just sorry, you to fat, your to ugly, your not smart enough. What ever you have ever heard to discourage you do well.

This side of your mind was kept in silence of all of the negative things that you once heard, this sound of your mind was like being in a sound proof room, it heard nothing negative. This is the we can make it happen side of your mind, so use it, it awaits you this is the green side where dreams come true, the soil is rich, what you plant is that one seed and you water it and watch it grow, there no need for a plan B because plan "A" the only one you need is guarteed to grow. Why? Because now you are at the point where you finally believe it's possible. If you believe and stick with it you know it's just a matter of time and your dream will come true. I truly believe that I can do all things threw Christ that strenthen me. See I have allowed my mind to stretch and allow myself to believe in me. When I once depend on some one else to think for me this I want do no more, I have a mind and I chose to use it to benefit me and my family and others I chose to help not limited to away of life that some one choose for me by punching a clock. To take control of my life and limit my money and the way I spend my money.

If I choose to use my mind and make my dream, come true then I want spend all of my value times working on keeping some one else dream in motion. If I should choose to allow my mind to be stretch for new ideal then I want have to worry about my future my kids and grandkids future one day they will follow the path I have laid before them.

If I choose to allow my mind to stretch and learn how to run my own business, then and only then will I be successful at running my own life and taking control of my destiny. If I choose to allow my mind to stretch it's then and only then will I be able to see my dream home that I all ways wanted, my bank accounts grow beyond measure, my grandkids get the best education that money can buy. Take the vacations that my wife and I, family deserve. I have to allow my mind to stretch so I can really have freedom in my mind and in my life. What is life if you are bound, with bills, no money no way to make money, dead in job and a naying spouse. This along is enough to drive a man or a woman crazy.

CHAPTER XLIII

MAKE EXCUSES OR MONEY

You have to make a choice which one you are going to do, it's and either or choice, you can't have your cake and eat it to. Either you spend your life making excuses why you can't do something or make up your mind to do it. It's almost just that simple it's your life so you decide, what you are going to do. People spend to much time making excuses why they can't get there self together. Why they can't go forward with there dreams. They want what others have made, but they don't want to go threw the fire. May they didn't get the memo there no one going to give you anything in this life time. Only salvation is free and even it take some work, the bible tell your faith with out work is dead. Success with out work is also dead meaning it's not going to happen. People that make money find ways to make money they follow there dreams, and they make good on them.

This is why I say you either make money or excuses they don't come in the same box. They come in two different boxes, choose the one you want to open they are labeled. There is no surprise! Don't spend your life talking about your past or what happen in the past when you can have a better future. See your past is just what it is your past, so let it die. So what your husband left you in debt, your wife left you broke. Your mom and dad were crack heads. It time out for that you are grown and now and the choices you make now depend on you. The choices yo make now is the choice you make for your future.

So yo can make excuses are you can make money, let your past die and your future live. You can make money only if you are stronger enough to go forward with your life. To follow your dreams and make something great happen. You now have the opportunity to be a living testimony, about how life gave you a bad hand and made something great out of it. Let your sad past be the reason for a better future, use that for level to go higher in your life, instead of a ditch to fall in. you have to learn to use every tool necessary to make your life a success your life a joy!

See you have to realize some times that something happen for a reason. And it up to you to make the best of a bad situation, in other words you have the power to turn the things around and make the best out of it.

People that want to really make money they really don't make excuses, they make money. Life is hard enough as it is don't make it harder with your excuses why you can't do something. Just keep one thing in mind and that is this, you will all ways work on a dream whether it's your are some one else.

If you can make your dreams bigger than you excuses, then you will soon be on the road of success. When you learn not to complain and instead take advantage of your opportunities, that come your way instead of making excuses. You'll get where you are trying to get faster. I tell people about opportunities that pass you by time and time again. Why! Because for some reason we are never positions, nor condition to take on a great opportunity when it come our way. Some time when a great opportunity come your way, that you can't let pass you by if you have to, if you have to borrow to make it happen.

I had to borrow money to get in the business that I got in, why because I saw a great opportunity that I did not want to pass me by. I thought to my self well I being borrow all my life for one reason are another, so why not borrow this time so I want have to borrow no more duh! So that what I did hey man let me borrow this money for about 45 day. I said forty five days because the business I was getting into 5 Linx Home Base Business it was said that I could make my money back in 30 days. I was one of the ones that took the challenge, and I did over double the money back in less than 30 days. So at this point all I had to do was wait on my money to pay this guy back.

Oh! And the company did send my money back, how much? Well the truth is being told. I spend less than $400.00 to get in the Business and less than 30days I had made $1000.00 back and that was just Bonus money for getting 2 other people to come in under me in my Business. That's right my business! Once you get into this Business you are the leader See there are great opportunity out there, all you have to do is quit being scared and trust your mind on something that you think about, other do and they do well. Quit making excuses and start making money! Again you can't do both it's either are, you going to make it for you are you are going to keep making it for the one that don't even know your name.

I remember working in all the different type of factory I worked in, I never like it and Lord know I hated in the suits walked threw, most time in a hurry. You would be working and it was like to some when I see some people try to speak to these guys, there heads where so high they couldn't hear them. To me I saw was a bunch of people working in the cotton field and master walk threw, and a few slave would look up and say morning BOSS! And he look as though he was saying get back to work. The only different was on this plantation there people of many colors watching as the Big Boss! Walked three.

I wasn't better than no one else I worked with by a long shot, but I would only speak if they spoke because I seen there kind for years so why waste my breath.

I guess I got my attitude from my old dad, he told me one day long before he died and it stuck with me. "He said son let me tell you something, I was in the Army for 23 years, worked at Fort Root as a cook for another 18 + years. I begged, borrowed, stole and gamble to make sure you guys was all right. And that he did! Then he looked at me and said for that reason, that very reason along there is no reason you have to kiss no man A** at all. And that stuck with me for years and that parts of the reason why it was hard for me to work for other people because they some time want me to do what I cant Kiss up to them! that's another reason why I live my his rule 'HAVE YOUR OWN & YOU CAN'T GET MAD ABOUT SOME ONE ELSE!

So I will close this chapter with you can! LIVE YOUR LIFE WITH MONEY! OR YOU AN LIVE YOUR LIFE WITH EXCUSES! YOU CAN'T HAVE BOT!

CHAPTER XLIV

BUILDING YOUR DREAM

You know we talk a lot about building our dreams, but there are some things that there going to take to make it happen! Lets take some time and go threw a few of them.

1. Time : it's going to take time, if you don't have can't find you might as well for get it right now. Because anything anyone sat out to do it take times, some times more time than you have, some time less time than you expected we just never know. So this is why we must put time in the plan and a lot of it.

2. Passion : you have to have passion for what you are doing, are you want make it you have to love what you are doing are trying to do. Take for instance I worked at t a community radio station for over 15 years, never got paid for what I do and yet I was good at it. Some people and some jocks say man how you do that for so long for no pay? Well I love what I do and I believed everything if you do it right and long enough is for a reason. Well like now over the years on me being on that Radio Show, people know me and trust me. Now I can tell them about my book free of charge and help get it out to the people. So that, that was free for them is now a profit for me. But most of all before I ever started to write this book, I had passion for being a radio announcer whether I got paid for it are not.

3. Why - Really may be this should have been the #1, Why! Do you want to do this? Why do you want this so bad! You know

most people that get in to business have a strong why! They want to do something and they keep that thought in mind and they become successful. Why? Because they remember there why! This is what we have to do to make thing happen, but some come into the business with this big why and before they get to where they say they want to go there why is no longer important. Man that really bother me, just being 100, weak people like that I really wish I never met. It may sound cruel, but that's just my opinion. Your why could be just that you want a better life, you are tired of making other folks rich, you want to take contro lof your life. What ever your WHY! IS PLEASE STICK TO IT!

4. Commitment : Be real with your self, be 100 with you if you couldn't do it with no one else. Promise yourself that I'm going to do this! I will make this happen! Look up and tell the Lord it's just you and me now. If you are with me who can be against me that matter? I hated when I see a person that can't be true to there self, and this is what I'm asking you to do for you be true to you. This is about you, only you can give your self the life style that you are looking for. Even if some one else gave it to you, that mean they have the power to take it away. But if you go and get it, it's yours.

5. Sacrifice : Find time when you don't have time, get rid of some of your friends. Get rid of the dead weight, no need to carry it around it /they are just in the way of your journey. I had to get rid of some of my buddies, I didn't call and say hey buddy I have to quite talking to you are nothing like that. I was just like a junky going cold turkey, I just quite calling are going over. I talk to them when I saw them and that was it. Not that I thought I was better are nothing like that. The point is I was on a mission and I needed nothing are no one in the way. At this point in my life you could help me are hurt me. If you couldn't help me them you were hurting me. So get rid of your buddies right now there's be plenty time for that when you make it to the top. Get rid of your tv, your music, your party time. Yes I'm saying take back all the time and extra time you can get why? Because you are going to need it. Let go now thing that you can have later. Just think if you

keep working 2/3 jobs you are not going to have time for all of these people and things any way duh!

6. Motivated : You have to be effected in what you are doing and what you believe, if you are in business and you are expecting some one to follow you in your venture. You must be motivated enough your self to get people to believe in what you are doing, you have to stay postive every day of the week about what you are doing and what you believe in. I learn there is no vacation sort of speak for people that are tring to make it to the top of there game, there is no time off. Every day is a work day toward a better future a better you. I was at a Wedding of my step son a little while back, after the vows and the eating took place.

    I was outside greeting the folks while they were leaving and handing out my business cards. You know you all ways have that smart butt, ask me not knowing who I was did I come to the wedding to see the wedding are past out business cards. I was like both to be a part of my step son wedding and past out business cards. She them looked and said so this guy is your step son? I was like ya! And the cards I'm passing out is my business cards. She looked at me crazy and I was like see that the problem with business that don't suceed, no one know that they have a business in some cases. Why because they want they advantage of a great opportunity when it presents it self. There was a crowd there and I took advantage of it, if I'm not motivated about what I'm doing and willing to be bold then he will do it for me.

7. Focus : What ever you do when you start on building you dream stay focus, there are a lot of distractions around you every day. There everything from you don't where to go, to haters don't want to see you go no where. So you have to stay focus at all times you have to believe in what you are doing and most of all WHY! You are doing it. You must at all times remember you are a winner, and you are great. There greatness in you just waiting to come out. If you can get yourself to focus ou will be surprise that you will come up with in a short time. There are going to be days maybe weeks even more it may look like you can't do, there no way it going to happen for you. I know because I been there. I just refused to get

old one day and can't do anything but whish I had tried a little longer. I think I open every door there was for success and when I thought I wanted to give up and say the heck with it. Lo and behold there was another door waiting on me to open. It was called 5 Linx HomeBase Business, when I pulled on the door and the door open and there it was something that I been looking for a long time SUCCESS!

8. PATIENCE : This is a must, if you don't have it you might as well stop right now and go back to what you are doing. It takes a lot of patience when you are trying to build a business. It not an over night thing, it takes time even if you got it up and running in a few months. It still takes time to build don't for get that, you have not build it yet you just open it. Don't let the fact that you open and had a grand opening look like every one showed up for what ever reason. Some come to buy some come to see, and it seem like the future is great and it might be.

     But don't fool yourself there still a lot of work to be done, one if you had a great opening some of those people you may never see again. So you have to build your trust, and have the attitude that you are in business and you need each other. What I'm tring to say is this that was just one day, you still have tomorrow to deal with and the day after.

9. Determination : Threw it all you have to be determine, to make this thing happen. A real dreamer dreams day and night, day time when thing are going well. Night times is when things are not going great but you are still able to keep your dream alive. This is really when no one else can see your dream but you, people that you started with will say heck no it's over. They think at this point we are just wasting our time and our just fed us and eventually walk away.

     Now it seem like the world is against you are there no one to talk to about this, because it been to long. All you want now is to crawl in a hole yourself and hate you ever came up with the ideal in the first place, but you know deep in side you can make it happen it's your dream you tell your self make it happen. The other side of you tell you ya! that's the problem its your dream. See this is where you have to walk at night to keep your dream alive, you have remind your self no one said it was going to be easy! But its possible! That we all the stuff you listen to and studied kick in Less Brown, E.T. The hip hop Preacher, and Tyler Perry, Will Smith, Steve Harvey. Oprah Winfrey and many other that you have listed to tell you it's possible. Now one time they said it was going to be easy but look at there struggle and they made it.

You have a mind and a dream and you can make it just like they did! If you are determined to not let nothing are nobody get in the way. So what it didn't come early but it came. And now because of your hard work and determination, your believeth you have prove again that any one can make it. You have over come your circumstances and achieve your goal and have Achieve Extraordinary success.

Now you have become a part of the team of Believers, the team that know first hand that is POSSIBLE! Your Dream Is Possible! It's Possible.

10. Putting God First! This really should have been number one and still is!

CHAPTER XLV

DREAM LIKE A LIGHT SWITCH

I see the problem with some people, there dreams are like the light switch in there homes. They turn them on one day and then the next day they are off. Meaning when things are going good they are hyped and want to tell the world about what they are trying to do. But when they things are not going so well in there life and there dreams are not going the way they like then they want to give up, in other words they are turning off the switch.

They are closing the curtain on there future there dreams, and you can't make it like that. You have to stay strong in the good days and the bad days, you have to push forward even when everything have stopped. Some time you have to push all by your self to jump start what you started all over again.

If you ever had an old standard shift car and the battery go dead in it, and it want start. So you would have to get in it, and hope you were by a hill so you could push in going down a little hill and jump start it. This was something you could do your self even if there was no one else around. This is the same way you have to do your dream even if there no one else around to help you get started, you have to push your dream forward and make it happen.

You are just wasting time and energy turning on and off the light switch. When you do this it's not only hard for people to believe in you, it will get to the point where you don't believe and when you stop believing in you then it over. See for years and years I have tried many things to make a difference and some times things went ok! And then there were times when I juts wanted to give up and just be the regular old Joe! You know life is funny even if I decided to just give up there was still a cost to pay there too.

See because one day in my life, if the Lord allow me to see it I was going to get old. And getting there are heading in that direction I was going to think about the things I should have done in life. I was going to be saying to myself what if? I would have kept working on my dream... what if! I would have done like many others no matter how long it took I stayed on it and made it happen? What if I would have work a little harder and believe a little more? What If! I would have stayed away from that light switch, just turned it on and left it along. Where I could have been today, now here I am wondering like many others, wondering what if! I would have left the light switch on and where I could have been today.

Please hear me! People one thing you don't want to live your life in WHAT IF! This will drive you insane all by itself. You have the power to change your life if you want to. You have the strength to turn on the light switch of ideal and greatness in your life, only if you will. Have the power to turn it on and the sense to leave it along. Instead of living your life being what I call the C.W. B. in life be what you can be and that successful many have done it and you can too.

God have given all of us a brain to use just like the next man, yes some may have been genus, and there was only a hand full of those. But the rest where the believers and the one that believe that they could do, and would not stop until it was done. You can't stop until you win... and even then you take a short breather and keep moving forward. Why because you have done something great and it feel good to you and you know it. You like the way it make you feel and you want more, because you know that you and God work good together and there more work to do and you want to do it.

Just think to your self before I turn a light switch off, I will turn another one on. Just to see what the end is going to be. The bible even let us know that a man can't walk in darkness he have to have light in the spiritual and in the nature. You must have light so the light that pops up in your head is a new and great ideal and yo have to keep it going to make it happen. Remember it's your dream so make it happen.

You have the right to right the story of the life time, the way it began it wasn't your fought but the way it end and the way you live out the middle it is. There is no way easy way to success no matter what you think. It is an acting that have to be worked on every day. Success is and action word that need to be worked on every day, when you are not putting your hands on it your mind should be o it, if you want it to happen. It's not just a thinking process it's a doing process, you have to do it to make it happen. Sometimes over and over again until you get it right, but if you believe you can you can. If you believe you can't you can't.

CHAPTER XLVI

TEMPORARY

The things that you are going threw are (or) should I say can be temporary! The things that we go threw from poverty, to sadness, stress, what ever you are going threw are just temporary if you want it to be. If not it can be fatal it can be that thing that take you out if you are not careful. We all have choices but what we do with them are on us, the way we live our life, the job we take, the educations, that we get we have a choice of what we can and want to do.

The problem is that we have choices but people want take them. They are so busy trying to find something wrong with the system, so they can have an excuse for there situation. Well I'm here to tell you to stop looking for something to be wrong with the system and look at the one in the mirror that the system is made of. It's up to you how you live and die and what in between, its up to you no one fought but yours if you fail in life no one fault but yours. Back in the day we if people were anything beside white Americans we blame the white man for our down falls and doing with out. You know they would are we would say it's the man fought. Meaning the man in office the president whom ever. "BREAKING NEWS "THE MAN IN THE OFFICE NOW IS BLACK" SO NOW WHAT?

But the great things even in those days, there were many they fought and got what they wanted in life. These were the dreamers the one that believe that the American dreams was good for all what ever there culture was.

Your situation was really temporary! You are the one that made it last by not doing nothing in your life to change it. This bring to mind some of the Temps service around the state. One in particular that I worked for, Don't get me wrong there are nothing wrong with them, but they are design to help get you back on your feet back into the work force. It's design for you to stay there for a while, get hired on at the particular job are move on. But they are 'TEMPORARY' jobs that why in most cases they don't pay much, and the reason why is to make you do better.

So tell me why in the world would a person take one of these jobs and stay there for 8/10 years why. They don't pay much, there no medical insurance, they get half of your pay check every week not just one week, and you never get a raise.

But you can't get mad at them because they are making money, and they told you that they were a "TEMPORARY SERVICE" meaning the job was just for a little while not a life time. BUT IF YOU WANT TO STAY!

When I had gotten one of these jobs and I heard that some had been there, for 6, 7, 8, 9 10 years. I was like either these people had low self-esteem are they were just lazy. If you are working to make money then how in the hell, can you stay on a job where you never get a raise?

We complicate our life and then we blame others, "THE MAN" these are some of the people that are complaining about every thing. But when you come up with a solution they get quite. When you tell them there is a better way and there is a light at the end of the tunnel they close there eyes and go back into there world of make believe and then say I'm all right.

I believe the greatest feeling in the world is when you succeed in something that you sat out to do. Knowing that what you was going threw was temporary and prove it by making something happen in your life as well as others. Being broke are homeless can be temporary! Living from pay check to pay check, can be temporary if you choose to make a difference everything that wrong in your life can be temporary if you are willing to change.

Remember one thing the way you came, in this life was not your fault! Your mom and dad may have done the best they could for you. But they were barely making it, you may have been a child that was giving away, didn't have a mother are father. Grew up poor and with out, etc. etc. those are not reason for you to be broke are homeless the rest of your life. Those are reason for you to get off you butt! And make a better you. Your situation is temporary unless you make it perm anted

CHAPTER XLVII

EXCUSES IS ABUSE!!

When you make excuses in you life you are abusing yourself and other that are in your life. "EXCUSES IS ABUSES" when other have done something and you say you can't do it because of! Of what? You didn't try? It very easy to make and excuse why something didn't go well in your life, instead of learning why something didn't go right and fix it you give up. You know if you are that person I feel very sorry for you. Because one because you will never make it with that way of thinking.

2 because you are abuse person to yourself, you beat up your self with excuses why something can't happen in your life. I could kind of understand if that which are trying to do have never been done before. But success is happening everyday in some one life.

Why not yours? No one is asking you to invent the wheel, just rode with the wheel that is all ready turning. You have the knowledge to do anything you want to these days. There are books you can read, you tube and internet services that can tell you about anything these days that you want to learn, if you want to learn!

So why make excuses to live the way you are living, the home you are living in that should be condemned, the car that want hardly run. You are not only abusing your self with the excuses you make to not try to do better, you are doing it to your kids and your spouse. You are hurting a whole generation if not two, there is not a reason for you to really do with out unless you are scare of trying. Life is truly about up and downs, but when you are already down in some cases the only way left is up.

But you have to be the bold one that step out and take that chance, to give your self a chance for a new you a new future. Things don't just happen! People make them happen not just by saying are talking they are doers. You have to be a doer, there no other way thing are going to change. Some one may hit the lottery that is reading this book but will that some one be you. Will that one in three hundred million be you?

Don't take that chance when I'm trying to show you an opportunity to become that million aire you always wanted to be, that person of wealth that you all ways wanted. Your dreams are possible here in this Business called 5 Linx Home Base Business go to my web-site. www.5linx.net/buildingdreams click on opportunity learn about the business join the business and lets talk… 501.442.6899 call me. Let me show you how to get to the next level. If I have to I will come to where you are, to make it happen build you a team. Which can make everyone money this is real! Do it for you and your family far off.

STOP! STOP! WITH THE EXCUSE & THE ABUSE! now before it's to late. STOP! PASSSING up Great Opportunities! STOP! Being afraid of success! You have made other people successful why not you. You have the ability to make other rich so why not use the same mind and do it for you.

What I'm saying is simple, when making up your mind to make something great happen. Just like going to work on a new job! You follow instruction that your boss give you and you make it happen. In this business we are in called 5 Linx the same thing applies. The different is you are the Boss, so that more reason to work harder with out the excuse & abuse.

What really get me about people is this, they are real smart when it come to helping other get and stay rich. We go in our best attire, with our best smile and say are you hiring. They look at you and smile and give you a application, what you are really saying not are you hiring, but "CAN I HELP KEEP YOU & YOUR FAMLY STAY RICH"

And they tell you ya! Sure you can! Now they have you lock in the Slave Camp for at least 40 hours a week. Sometimes longer and before you know it you are there 10 years. But remember you were going to stay just a little while and go to school are something of that nature and get out of there.

But while you were there you were making bill after bill, and you never went to school are did nothing you had plan. Now you have 20 years in the "SLAVE CAMP" even if you wanted to leave you are bounded down. But you are still talking about getting out, but every one that know you know that you are just talking. You have now giving the company 30 years in there "SLAVE CAMP" You have worked hard now to keep Mr. Mrs. Bug Bug! The Master rich and the bad part about it they don't even Know you still after 30 years you never saw the Boss! But you kept him rich now you are getting close to retirement and you been talking about it for awhile.

At least you think that part of your dream will come true, but you have bought a house finally late in your life. A new car after driving a used one for years and when you think about it you can't retire, you need a little more time. The sad part now they have used you and got as much out of you as possible, so now you finger hurt all the time, your back hurt, you all ways going to the doctor. So they are now subjecting that you go on out a little early (retire) you have a few more years yet.

You figure you can do it, but they say a few of you have to take the early retirement are be fired! "GRATITUDE" HUH! If though you were foolish enough to do this for all these years, work on some one else dreams and not yours even though you had some good ones. But you fail to act, 'BECAUSE" great reason why! 'BECAUSE' you were scared to complete an assigement that God had gave you to do.

But now yo wish you had followed your mind, and not let others tell you what you couldn't do. Now you wish yo had listen when you heard some one say that it was possible. Now you wish you had listen when you heard some one say, others had did it you can too.

But in stead you had excuses why, and you were going to wait until things got better in the mean time you just abused your self all those years just thinking things were going to get better all by themselves. Now look at you with your head down trying to play like life is going to be good now, you don't have to get up until yo get ready. You tell your co - workers ya life is really going to be good now ya! It's going to be GREAT! Deep inside while you say that, you are thinking about the house you still have 20 years on, the new car you still have over 3 years on plus the others bill you have made.

To top it all off you were having problem paying it with the check, you were making and now you are going to only have a 3rd of it, and all your bills. But you know you can't afford to stop working but you have no choice. They tell you to retire are be fired so! Since you mommy didn't raise no fool, you took the early retirement. There was a time they use to give you a gold plated watch and a party. But now the ones who knew you said good bye and good luck with a smile and went back to work.

You were now released from the "SLAVE CAMP" with there blessing in the real world. You stay off a month or two not really enjoying your retirement, because your bills are piling up. So what you do you go back in the work field and find a job, working 40 hours a week in pain. 'THE SLAVE CAMP' until one day you go to break tired and broke down still chasing that $.

Everybody go back to the line but you, you are still sating there. After about 20 minutes some one miss the old man. So they look in the bath room and then some one looked in the break room and there you were. You were just sitting there and your worker call out to you come on old timer. You sat there like you heard nothing, and then the guy call out again, come on old man before the boss come get you 'THE MASTER" You just sat there and finally the guy come around and look at you. He shake you because you look like you are sleep! Wake up old man before you get fired!

And then your life less body slump down in the seat, it hard to fire an man that just "expired" Where you took your last breath! You have finally worked yourself to death. You died where you lived on the job! Chasing after money instead of your dreams!

PLEASE DON'T LET THIS HAPPEN TO YOU! BECAUSE IT CAN!
AND IF YOU ARE NOT CAREFUL IT WILL.

We are all going to leave here one way are another one day, true enough but while you are here lets enjoy the life the Lord gave us. Lets use the mind that he given us to be different, some people are maybe put here to work as they do. But I believe you are not one of those people. You know you are not, you come to far in this book for me to believe you are not a believer in yourself and your thought, your vision, your dreams. So stop making excuses and stop abusing your self and lets make something happen. If not for you think about your family and what you are able to do for them by you stepping out and believing in you! Remember (1) God First (2) Family (3) NOW DO YOUR BUSINESS….

CHAPTER XLVIII

BE SURE OF YOU!

There come a time in your life when you have to get out of the shadow, and be the person. You have to learn how to be what you Wanna be and not be afraid of what can happen. How can you ever know if you don't try how can you tell some one else to do something you want do or afraid to do.

I remember I went to check on a job at a company to drive a fork lift. when I applied for the job after the lady read over my application, she asked me would I consider a Supervisor job? I was like I had never been a supervision before, in other words I was use to been told what to do other than telling some one what need to be done.

I guess she saw something in me that I didn't see. So she said here's what we will do. You put on your application forklift / supervisor. So when you go and have an interview they will see that you are flex able, she smiled and say what will it hurt they can only say yes are no. I was like cool so they call me in for an interview, One white guy Brad and the other was a black guy Reggie.

Both of these guys were big guys, put they seem cool and down to earth, I liked that about them. Now the Reggie was a little odd the black cat, why I say that because this guy was wearing and still wearing his singature safety glasss which where white. Dude was darker than me, ok tell it like it is blacker than me big with these white frame glasses. I thought to myself just maybe this guy one time are another played for George Clinton of Parliament Funk A Delic are something.

But on the real they were both cool glad I meet both of these guys, we talked for a while and Brad then said on your app. I see you want a forklift /Supervisor job, I kind of chicken out for a moment at that point and said the lady at the office told me to put it like that. I just want to be a fork lift driver, he looked at me and said you know the fork lift job is kind of fast paste. I thinking to my self now this guy just called me an old fart. I was about to get in my old feeling and asked what you trying to say?

He then played it off and said I don't mean you cant do it, but looking at your app. I think you have enough experience to be a Supervisor what you think? Boy it was time to roll play now, look like the fort lift job was out so I better play along are be along. This where all of those motivated tapes I been listening to come in handy. Before I could think my mouth say ya! I can do it! I had to remember what I tell people all the time 'OPPORTUNITY NEVER STOP KNOCKING, BUT IT WILL PASS YOU BY! AND THAT WHAT YOU LET PASS YOU BY SOME ONE ELSE WILL SEE COMING"

In other words they needed a supervisor and some one was going to get the job, whether it was me are some on else. Why not me! opportunity is knocking baby let it in.

He ran me threw a couple of question about how to handle situations when they come. Again listening to people like Les Brown, ET, Eric Thomas and others I knew I could make it happen even if I had to fake my way threw it for a while. I thanks these guys for given me the opportunity. Most of all I THANK GOD! FOR OPENING THIS DOOR FOR ME TO STEP IN TO NEW TERRORITY!

See I had to come to the reality I could do this, if others trust you to do something,why cant you trust your self to do it. Learn to be sure about you! Have a postive attitude about your self. We have to keep in our mind if others can do it I can too! After being told what to do after 30, 40, years of my life what to do it should be simple to tell and guide others.

Just do what others have taught you if you were paying attention, after all these years it call duplication what are ready been done. But been better than you have been taught, it very easy I found out to work with most people that want to work. I learned if I come in with a good attitude others will have one, simple hey how are you to day! Telling them they did a good job when they have! Letting them know you appreciate them and what they are doing for the team. I have to say 98% of my days and working with others are good if not great.

I mention duplication and that what life is really all about, duplication what all ready been done. Michael Jackson didn't create the moon walk he just duplicated what he saw done before and mastered it. Because he was know all over the world just about he took it to the people and mastered it. The one that started it had very limited source so know one knew what he really had done. So what ever you do in life in other words I'm saying it's all ready been done. So just make and do it better and get paid more for what you have done.

It all go back to been sure about you, been postive about you stepping out and taking the challenge that life throw at you. Either you will hit the ball or strike out, even the ones that struck out had another chance at the bat. By this time they were ready, when they swung this time the ball was knock out of the park HOME RUN!! BABY! But you have to be sure of you and be ready for the next time! So when the opportunity come you can strike out or knock it out of the park. Life in what you make of it, when you want something you work for it, and hard. Keep in in mind no one is going to give you nothing, if you want it you have to go for it for your self.

The great thing about making something happen in your life is this, when you make it happen you will apprecitae it more. Knowing you can make something happen great in your life make you want to make something else happen. Then you realize you can do it again and again, man that deserve a WOW!

CHAPTER XLIX

YOUR LIFE

I see to many people in life that have really just have given up, people that just don't seem to care to more. They work dead inn jobs with no future, some are working jobs that don't even give them a raise. I mean for real, 4 real? For 4 real? Come on really that's really a case of low or no self-esteem.

Help me understand this I thought the reason you work was to make money, and to make much as you can. So this why I can't understand why people will just settle for so long and just give up hope. Some people just believe in what there are doing is ok! That what they think any way or say, but the reality is they are not happy. They are just afraid to get out of the box, and be reprogram to a better way of life. They know that there is something better but they are afraid of getting out of there comfort zone.

They realize if they decide to do something different it may just cause for a little more effort than they are willing to give. More time of themselves and being more productive and caring than they want to, Your life is easy when you are working for some one else, but not as rewarding if it was you making the money that some one else work for. See all they had to do was to come up with the ideal and believe and then put it in motion. Once the plan started to work then some one else could do the job, that's business in most cases.

They come up with the ideal and the money and put you to work. They make millions and the little man makes hundreds. Wow! What a great system we have, but don't hate because they whom ever they may be wasn't scared to make the challenge, stretch there mind and let something great enter into it. The great thing about this is you and I can do the same thing. If we would just stop fearing something that can't bite nor hurt you! Words that come out of other people mouth. Words that are not true unless you make them come true. They are just what they are words and other opinion of you.

I remember Jerry Butler sang a song when I was coming up! ONLY THE STRONG SURVIVE! Oh how true only the strong will make it in any type of business, you can't be as my Pastor use to say Bishop Lodes Warren "A JELLY BACK" back just bending all kinds of way. Just bend to anything and every thing, some where down the line you have to stand up and be a man /women.

Other people bad opinion are thoughts should not matter, at all to you. They are just what they are opinion they are there's and mean nothing to you. That's the way you have to see things when you are trying to make something happen in your life, and when people try to stop you. Lets go a head and call them what they are, HATEING DEVILS! See when the Lord go to work the devil do, everything that is possible to make your dream a night mare if you let it.

The great thing about being successful is other people have done it, and you can too. Other people have made there dreams come true and you can too. Might of fact just think about it you are so great you have been helping some one else dream come true for years. Getting a little pay and no for your effort, while they get all the credit and the pay. If you are part of the 40 / 40/ 40 plan and you are ok with it great, shut this book and go get your sleep and go to work building some one else dream. Now let me explain the 40/40/40 plan. Here's the deal you work on your job 40 hours a week, 40 years are more, retire and get 40% of you pay that you work so hard for all of your life. Oh! Ya that might as well add another 5/10 so years, why? Because those are the years when you have to go back to work when the retirement, pay is not enough.

That's the American way if you want to believe that and work for some one else all your life.

But if you are really real about getting out of debit and staying out, sating goal for you and your family. Having a college fund for your kids, been able to take vacation as long as you want. Go to work on your own time instead of some one else. Not waiting to get old to enjoy your life when you can enjoy it now tomorrow is not promise do I need to say more? Conquer your Fear and do your Business and make some great things happen in your life and you can. 5 Linx, want you but you need a Business like 5 Linx Home Base Business! www.5linx.net/buildingdreams

If you cant be my Business Partner then do be a favor and become my customer. Check out the products and save money by buying from my web-site. If you need one of our products please buy from my site…. God Bless You!

CHAPTER L

BE STRONG & SURVIVE

Life is funny sometimes and not so funny others times. See when people try to make a change in there life there are all ways challenges to be met. Whether it's friend, family are strangers they are right there waiting on you. Some one are something that will all ways try to turn you back. Here's the deal they don't see what you see, and so they want believe in what you believe and they want see it until you have the money in your hand. By the way remember it's your dream and your vision God gave it to you there was no one else there when he put it in your spirit. So you have to be strong and run with it are be weak get tackled and never get up again and run.

See when I talk about being successful are rich, people find something wrong with that, they try and make you feel bad for wanting something better for you and your family and other that you can help. It's hard to help any one if you are broke, if he hungry and on the street and he asked you for a dollar are 2. Well you might say you don't have to be wealthy are rich to do that and you are absolutely correct.

But that is small thinking on your part because, I would like to do more than that. I like to be able to donate to the hungry in a big way, to St. Jude Hospital in a Big way for the great work they have done threw the years, the Ark. Children Hospital for the Great work they have done threw the years. It's not all about me or a few people I see broke on the streets, it's about others organizations that are helping thousands in what they are doing if I could donate to these organizations that are helping kids and adults. This is why I want it so bad and have a better life for me and my family. Now what's your W-H-Y?

So I can't and want feel guilty about wanting better in life than what I have. I realize something in life a long time ago, that is people are like robots. It's as though they are trained to do one thing as they grow up and that's work for other to help keep them stay rich. Sad part about it we do a real good job of it from the cotton fields to the factory we are so awesome on keeping others rich and wealthy. It's seem as though some time we think if we stop working for others and take care of our own it's a crime. The sad part about it is, we are the only one that feel that way, why?

We seem to think if we are not working the 40 hrs foe some one else we are not going to make it. But I the same time you work the forty for someone else you are not making it. You still have to fine a part time job are some type of hustle to make it I know I did it for years. So not only was I was still broke I was breaking down my body, using pills to stay awake week to sleep, cocaine to stay alert when I really needed to keep moving. See you didn't know this did you, being broke can casue some others problem trying not to stay broke. Working sometimes 50 plus hours on a job a week. Then working a part time job cleaning business or throwing news papers, had to find ways to keep going and when I got paid something would come along and I was still broke.

You have to realize you can't really get where you want to get by hitting a clock, why because it's not for not! It's to control you, to keep you at a certain level in life poor! Are just between poor and barely enough. People that have you hitting there clock need your service duh! So there fore they are going to let yo make enough money to get you by not rich! If every one got very wealthy are rich by doing so they would never keep no one on the job for a period of years.

CHAPTER LI

40/40/40 PLAN

This is the plan that over 98% of people fall into, working 40 hours a week, 40 years of you life and then getting 40% of what you made over your life span when you retire. Think about it if you barely making it now and you bills are growing monthly and your pay check was only growing once a year at 2%. Well by the time you retire your bills are so high and now you are only making 40% of what you was making that now have you more in debt.

Why because now yo are making 60% less than you were making and you still have the same bill plus some more, and you suppose to be happily retired no way unless you are a fool. Be real with your self, you can't do what you all ways said you would do when you retire. Sat out side on the porch swing and have a nice ice tea or beer, maybe you can the first six months are so but after that?

You have to go back to work it's a proven fact now yo have to work until near death. I see it every day people retired to new jobs, brother and sisters don't let this be you nor I. I don't know where your mind is but mind is not about working when I said I'm retired I want to be retired and that's it. I want to be able to do what I want to do and need to and that's not to go back and hit some one clock another forty hours a day.

I use to hear people talking about retiring and sating on the front porch doing nothing. Playing with the grand kids, traveling etc. Ya! That was the dream man its sound good to one day that day came, and you got that day you were looking for retirement. Ya! Traveling, sating on the porch chilling and playing with the grandkids. Ya! You now have all of that but not the way you planned it. You now are traveling every morning to a different job, because you retired from the other one and they can't use, use you no more. Yes you are now playing with the grand kids if you are not to tired when you get of your new job. Oh ya! You sating on the front porch because you have worked hard all day like you were 30 again but you are not. You are 66 years old and you so tired you think if I can just make it to the porch, I'll be all right thank God, you made it there.

So now you sat there tring to catch your breath again, another day on your front porch tired. Life sometimes don't come out the way we plan, why because we don't plan.

We think we got it made because we have what we think is a good job so we turn are death if from any other opportunity that may come our way. But then this day come and you wish you had listen when guys like my self tried to show you a better way.

Don't be fooled by the life and what it may have for you, the sat up to the let down. Bottom line it's no one fault but your if you don't plan your future. People that you work for plan there future and there future is to have you to work for them as long as you are able to keep there dream alive and when you can't then? Well you know I'm sorry but we don't need you no more. You work for a place all of those years and you will think at least the son or daughter that you help raise will come down and see you off. Don't hold your breath, if you did you would die on that job instead of the next one.

The truth be told the only reason you are broke in this day in time is because you want listen. Sometime people are just program to be stupid, I had a broke man tell me he had enough money. I was like man where did you come from Mars, yes you have a little Janitoral service that doing well true enough. But what happen when the big company like Service Masters come in and bid on the jobs that you have and you are out in the cold. Will you have enough to hold you over for a periods of years perhaps?

Bill Gates, The Walton and many others Billion airs are still trying to make more money. This guy was just a thousand airs (lol) but you have enough money for who just you? What about others in your family that you can help if you made more. What about the legacy you leave behind one day for your kids. I mean if you have a business and you are out there killing yourself working the business then you have a way to go.

See most successful people that run successful business have other in charge to run there business. They come in we they need to or want to they are not there every day being worried with a lot of employees. That big business to me, not when you have to come in and mop a floor. You are still in the need of making more money.

All I'm trying to say is this there are no longer job security, no matter if you go to college are not. It's just not there you went to college and so did the one that want your job. They are young and fresh hyped just like you use to be and willing to work and at a cheaper price to get in the door. They are full of ideals and you have had one in years and the company needs new bright you guys and girls and you are about over the hill. So why put up with you any longer when I can get this person that have many years ahead of him/her if the Lords say the same.

All you are talking about is retiring, so they help you and now you feel mistreated because you gave these guys your all. You were talking about retiring but may 8-10 years from now not next month. See after they have worked like a Hebrew slave over the years now you are getting sickly. Going to the doctor all the time missing work in the Hospital a few times missing work, slowing down don't have it like you use to. The company need new ideals you have not thought of one in years.

Because you think your life is all right ya! You been around so long the guys in the big office love you. The guys in the big office trying to keep there money flowing too.

So now some adjustments have to be made and you are a part of it, it's you they have to let go with a few others. Nothing personally really, you may take it that way but its now believe me it is just business. Can't keep paying you if you have now ay of helping the company to make money. They think to there selves I can hire 3 more people at the price I'm paying him/her, it's just business.

A business you are no longer a part of so there you are. Day after day I think and repeat what my daddy all ways said 'HAVE YOUR OWN SON' 'HAVE YOUR OWN' Business money what ever it may be if its your, it's yours.

That what I like about this Business of 5 Linx, being your own Boss and taking control of your life. Can't no one fire me but me and there are days I, will fire my self and take a vacation and come back look in the mirror and asked myself can I have my job back? I will look at myself and say ok! But quite again I, might not hire you back the next time.

CHAPTER LII

YOUR NAME ON THE BUILDING

Some companies have a way to make you believe, that one day you are going to be sitting in there seat. You will be the man beside the man, think about it, my friend there is no way they will give the seat up for you are any one else.

They make you feel like they can't do with out you and want you to believe it. There are hundreds of people just standing in line to do what you are doing. Here's the real deal unless your name is Junior you want be the CEO! Of that business.

Just like where you stay at, there are many building that have name on them. And when that person pass away the name will still be there, "BUT" and some one in the family will be taking over it and it want be you. Some of us had been with companies so lone you think our name should have been on the business. But not by a long shot there will be a spouse, a son, a daughter a cousin and are least some one in the family with the same last name.

I heard a question asked in a meeting one time, and that was do you know your great, great, great, grandfather? Everyone looked around and then said is this a trick question are what. The guy smiled and asked the question again and we replied no! he said do you know why? The answer was because he didn't leave you nothing, if he had you would remember him. See Michael Jordan, The Wal-marts grand kids and generation of kids will know him why because he would, have left them with a Legacy and some money and lots of it. Don't get mix up in life with do nothing people, if they are do nothing people and you hang around them you will be the same do nothing person. REMEMBER THE OLD SAYING, THE BIRDS OF THE SAME FEATURES FLOCK TOGETHERS. IT'S TRUE.

Each day of your life you need to wake up and thank the Lord for another day and then start to work on your Life, your business. Don't leave her one day and broke and your family in debt that you left behind. If you have a great ideal please run with it, if there a stranger at the red light run it. People love living there life keeping up a lot of mess. Not you see you are special and you want something out of your life and this is why you made it this far in this book. You want something out of life, you want to live life on the edge and with money in your pocket. If you fall yo will have a safety net to catch you. You will be the one that break the broke cycle in your family.

You will be the one that stand out, in your family because you have courage! Enough to do so and one day and one day soon you will be so proud of your self why! Because you hung tough and believe that nothing was to impossible for God and you! So yo have now become the Business man the Business woman that you all ways wanted to be and to prove you will soon be getting ready to move into that Busines office you all way wanted and the great thing about it just wasn't an office.

It was a building with your name on it!

CHAPTER LIII

STOP BEING CAUTION

Stop being afraid of going after your dream, stop being afraid of doing what you want to do in life. Once you realize that the biggest reason you are not successful is you. Not because of what you don't have, but more less want you have and don't use. The fact that you read this book close to the end tells me that you are a person that want more. You are a person that not satified where you are in life.

A person that know that better awaits you and you know it. So take of the breaks the go after your dream full force ahead. See greatness is right there at your finger tips. So have to get off the side line and get into the game, get off the bench and get into the game. You know there's nothing like winning, you know there's nothing like winning a game. But the truth is really there nothing like winning a game and you played in that game and took part in it. You wasn't on the bench, nor were you in the bleaches. You were in the game and took part of the winning, that was taking control of your life is like.

That why you have to go after your dreams with brakes off, for sure you may fail but failing only bring you closers to success. Believe me I know!!

CHAPTER LIV

DISCOVERING YOU!

When you find yourself and really start discovering yourself, you will find your self in a cross road sometimes. Between friends and family, love ones and relationships..some are found to be toxic at times and good to you but not good for you.

Example there was a point in my life when I was really trying to make it. At the point of starting a new adventure in life. Which took up a lot of my times, at the same time I found myself falling in love, which also so took up a lot of my time.

So there for I had to realize what was important to me and what would last. she and I got so close that she wanted me to be with her every moment, when I was off work.

I even tried hard to do that, but when I was just sating around the house with her doing nothing but making love and holding hands after wards. I realize I needed to be out making my business come true. There was something I needed to be doing.

I needed to be talking to people trying to get the wheel turning in my business. She said she understood but she didn't. every time I went to do the business she was mad are something. Or was trying to give me a time limit to get back to the house.

This was just draining me both ways sexually and mind. I was actually in love with this lady. If I, would have met letter in life we may have been together now. But there I was at a cross road in my life something had to give. I remember getting in an argument with this woman and she called me a broke ass nigga!! that what made the light come on in my mind and remember what my dad all ways told me.

Son all ways make your money as long as you had a job you can all ways get a woman. So it was at that point I had to let it go. If you calling me this, you must really want a man with money Duh!

I didn't have none and wasn't going to have none as long as I was lying between her legs and holding her hands all day.

Keep me broke and some guy with money or future come along and take you away and leave me all messed up. Even though I loved that lady very much I, also loved my dream of making something out of my self. In reality a dreamer will never let nothing get in his way of success. I rather die lonely knowing I tried, than give up my dream and live miserable. Rather die been a have been, than die knowing I could have and never tried. Bottom line if it's in the way move it, things, friends, love, relationships. If it not working with you its working against you. There was a song I use to like called "LOVES HURT" which is so true and the same time so do "BEING BROKE"

GOOD BYE TO "BUT"

It's time, yes it's time to say good bye to your excuses! It's time to take it to the grave once and for all. After the eulogy we will go to the grave site and get rid of it for ever. The friends of "BUT" need to be laid to rest also, so let's role play for a moment. Let's go to the place where we will start to lay this problem down, the choir will sing the song .... BUT IS TO SEAT ON NOT TO RELY ON... THAT WILL BE THERE FIRST SELECTION THE 2ND ONE WILL BE ....GET BUT OUT OF YOU LIFE SO YOU CAN LIVE...

We will allow a 2 minute talk on "But" if you like to tell how "But" cause a problem in your life.

Well there was a business man that stood up with tears in his eyes. He said he was a contractor and well known in the business. He said he remember when he bided on a job that he knew he was to get, all he had to do was bid. He said he filled out the bid for the job, that was worth a lot of money and was going to ready but his business in the black.

So he filled out the bid and the next day he was going to make sure the bid was in. "But" he said he put it in his desk, to mail it of the next day" but" for got about it. He had gotton so busy. Said he really didn't know what he was thinking at the time because this was really a big contract. Then one day low and behold something come in the mail about the bid. He then he remembered he hadn't mail and so with out opening up the mail, he ran to the mail box and mailed the bid.

It was after that is when he looked in the mail that was sent to him and saw that the bid had been given to another business down the street. He said at that point he was about to loose his mind, because the guy down the road bided $50.000.00 more than he did and he could have got the bid, "BUT" he forgot to send it in.

See we are going to have to put the word "But" to rest in out life. This little word has cost us time money, careers, life sort of speak.

Then a lady walked up and said you know I, all ways wanted to start my own Business, I knew I could do it. I had the skills and the know how to do it "BUT" I let my husband at the time talk me out of it. I let him convince me it was too much work and money to spend on it. He then did said you have a good job we are doing all right so why worry. "WE GOOD" A few years later her job left the country and she had to spend off her saving and 401K. And when all that was about gone and she still hadn't found the job to support her like they were use to.

She lost her husband too, and to a woman that was running her own business and he was helping her. Then she said I shouldn't have listen to this guy, "But "I did!

Here's the thing about life and that is nothing really last for ever. Especially a job here today and gone tomorrow, you just don't know. But one thing for sure if you build your own success you want have to rely on no one else. So let bury all of the excuses today, let "BUT" stay behind you not in front where.

We have to get rid of our excuses if we want to make it in this life, "But" is just a sad and bad way to live your life. My God get rid of the things that are in your way and make some great things happen in your life we are all capable of doing better if you want. I learn to laugh at people that say I can't do some thing and go ahead.

Don't spend time trying to show them that you can, just go for it. People shave away of slowing you down are stopping you if you, listing to what they have to say are think. I remember being a family gathering and I was proud of what I was about to do.

That I was getting ready to shoot a commerical for my Radio Show "Building Dreams"

I thought it was a good time to shine by letting the family know I was trying to so something positive in my life. Before I could get it out of my mouth good here come the negative thought. My sister said oh! No one listening that channel that you going to be on.

You're just wasting your money, this is the very reason why I just decided I want tell no one what I'm do just do it. Family members are normally one that shot you down. Then the friends and other come and finish you off.

AT THE END WERE GOING TO BURY BUT,

Printed in the United States
By Bookmasters